M·E·N·U · M·A·S·T·E·R·S

HIGH FIBRE MEALS

EDITED BY
JENNI FLEETWOOD

OCTOPUS BOOKS

MENU MATCH CODE

To allow more flexibility within the menus we have added
bold numbers after certain recipes to offer suitable
alternatives.
Thus, if the numbers ·3·11·14· appear after a starter, they
indicate that the starter of Menu 3, 11, or 14 could be
substituted.
Using the MENU MATCH CODE you will be sure to find
a menu to suit all tastes.

NOTES

Standard spoon measurements are used in all recipes
1 tablespoon – one 15 ml spoon
1 teaspoon – one 5 ml spoon
All spoon measures are level
Where amounts of salt and pepper are not specified, the
cook should use her own discretion.
Canned foods should not be drained, unless so stated in the
recipe. For all recipes, quantities are given in metric,
imperial and American measures. Follow one set of
measures only, because they are not interchangeable.

Jacket photograph: Deep-Dish Vegetable Pie, Lettuce and
Orange Salad, Red Fruit Salad

First published 1986 by
Octopus Books Limited
59 Grosvenor Street, London W 1

© 1986 Octopus Books Limited

ISBN 0 7064 2542 1

Produced by Mandarin Publishers Ltd
22a Westlands Rd
Quarry Bay, Hong Kong
Printed in Hong Kong

C · O · N · T · E · N · T · S

I·N·T·R·O·D·U·C·T·I·O·N

The idea of entertaining can be intimidating. Some of the best cooks, who regularly turn out marvellous meals for their families, pale at the prospect of cooking for guests.

It's the timing that's the trouble. How do you ensure that everything is ready when it ought to be? What if you forget something vital? How can you be certain the evening will be as trouble free as you can make it?

The answer, as with so many things, lies in the planning. Work out your menu well in advance, bearing in mind your guests' tastes, availability of ingredients and your pocket.

Try to balance colours, textures and flavours. If you plan a rich main course, think about a simple dessert such as a sorbet.

Cook ahead where possible. If you know the starter and dessert are safely stored in the refrigerator or freezer you can give all your attention to the main course and accompaniments.

Make yourself a timetable, then imagine you are eating the meal and work your way through the timetable to make sure there's nothing you've forgotten.

In this book we've done all the hard work for you. Here are fifteen marvellous menus for all occasions. The emphasis is on healthy eating and each menu is high in fibre. In the introduction to each menu we give helpful advice about setting the scene, and the countdowns for each meal ensure nothing is forgotten.

As you gain confidence you can mix and match dishes from the different menus (look for the number coding at the end of each recipe). Above all, relax and enjoy yourself.

⸘M·E·N·U⸘

· 1 ·

After-theatre Supper for 4

Garlic Mushrooms
Quick Brown Bread

·

Turkey Liver Kebabs
Spiced Cabbage Salad

·

Dried Fruit Compote

After an early show, there's nothing nicer than bringing friends home for a good meal. If the show was a disaster, you can tear it to bits over cocktails – if it was a success, you can bask in reflected glory.

Keep It Light

We've chosen a light meal in view of the lateness of the hour. Most of the preparation may be done early in the day, leaving you free to arrange the flowers, decorate the table, chill the wine *and* get yourself ready for a night out.

Totally Flexible

There's nothing to spoil if extra curtain calls delay your departure from the theatre. Your starter can be on the table within 15 minutes of your oven heating up and you can use the waiting time for a couple of minor last-minute preparations. For our countdown, we've assumed you return from the theatre about 9.15 pm. Dinner is therefore scheduled for 10 pm but you can easily adjust the timing to suit yourself.

One final point – don't let your guests guzzle chocolates during the show. This meal is far too good for dulled appetites!

Garlic Mushrooms

Metric/Imperial	American
2-3 cloves garlic, peeled and crushed	2-3 cloves garlic, peeled and crushed
125 g/4 oz butter, softened	1/2 cup softened butter
salt	salt
freshly ground black pepper	freshly ground black pepper
1 tablespoon chopped parsley	1 tablespoon chopped parsley
24 mushrooms, stalks removed	24 mushrooms, stems removed
a little extra melted butter	a little extra melted butter

1. Blend together the garlic, butter, salt and pepper to taste and the chopped parsley. Spoon the mixture into a piping (pastry) bag, fitted with a large piping nozzle (tip).
2. Brush the mushrooms with a little melted butter and arrange in four ovenproof dishes stem end up. Pipe the garlic and butter filling into each mushroom cavity.
3. Cook in a preheated oven (200°C/400°F), Gas Mark 6 for 10 minutes. ·9·10·

1. Sift the flour, salt and sugar into a mixing bowl and rub (cut) in the fat.
2. Blend the yeast with the warm water and leave in a warm place until the yeast has dissolved and the mixture is frothy.
3. Add the yeast liquid to the flour all at once. Beat with a wooden spoon into a fairly soft dough, adding more water if necessary.
4. Turn on to a floured board and knead well for 10 minutes. Stretch the dough to fit a large tin (pan). Fold in three or roll up and put into the warmed and greased tin. Place in an oiled polythene (plastic) bag and leave to rise in a warm place until it reaches the top edge of the tin.
5. Brush with slightly salted water and bake in the centre of a preheated oven (230°C/450°F), Gas Mark 8 for 15 minutes.
6. Reduce the heat to (200°C/400°F), Gas Mark 6 and cook for a further 30 to 40 minutes according to size. When cooked the loaf will shrink slightly from the tin. Test by tapping the bread base – it should sound hollow.
7. Remove from the oven and cool. ·11·

Quick Brown Bread

Metric/Imperial	American
500 g/1 lb wholemeal flour or 250 g/8 oz wholemeal flour and 250 g/8 oz strong white flour	4 cups wholewheat flour or 2 cups wholewheat flour and 2 cups white bread flour
2 teaspoons salt	2 teaspoons salt
1 teaspoon caster sugar	1 teaspoon superfine sugar
25 g/1 oz white vegetable fat or butter	2 tablespoons vegetable shortening or butter
15 g/1/2 oz fresh yeast or 2 teaspoons dried yeast and 1 teaspoon sugar	1/2 cake compressed yeast or 2 teaspoons active dry yeast and 1 teaspoon sugar
approx. 350 ml/12 fl oz warm water	approx. 1 1/2 cups warm water

Turkey Liver Kebabs

Metric/Imperial	American
2 courgettes, thickly sliced	2 zucchini, thickly sliced
250 g/8 oz small button mushrooms	2 cups small button mushrooms
juice of 1 lemon	juice of 1 lemon
125 g/4 oz streaky bacon, rinded, halved and rolled	4 bacon slices, halved and rolled
250 g/8 oz turkey liver, cubed	1 cup cubed turkey liver
freshly ground black pepper	freshly ground black pepper
ground paprika	ground paprika
chopped basil	chopped basil
olive oil	olive oil
salt	salt

1. Sprinkle the courgettes (zucchini) and mushrooms with the lemon juice.

2. Thread the courgettes, mushrooms, bacon rolls and turkey liver alternately on 4 long wooden skewers.

3. Season with pepper, paprika and basil and brush with oil. Cover and marinate in the refrigerator for 1 to 2 hours if possible.

4. Cook under a preheated grill (broiler) for about 10 minutes, turning occasionally until brown and crisp.

5. Season the turkey liver kebab skewers lightly with salt and serve immediately with warm toast and fresh tomato sauce.

Turkey liver kebabs

Variation:

Kebabs are ideal for entertaining. They are quick to prepare and extremely versatile. Try the following combinations of meat with fresh or dried fruits. Cubes of lean lamb with apricots and courgettes; chicken livers with apple wedges and sage; bite-sized pieces of chicken with prunes and bacon rolls.

The kebabs will be better if they can be marinated for at least 1 hour, or preferably overnight. Remember to preheat the grill before starting to cook the kebabs. Brush with any excess marinade as they cook.

Spiced Cabbage Salad

Metric/Imperial	American
1 young green cabbage, or 500 g/1 lb young spring greens, finely shredded	*1 young green cabbage or 1 lb young collard greens, finely shredded*
salt	*salt*
75 g/3 oz seedless raisins	*½ cup seedless raisins*
freshly ground black pepper	*freshly ground black pepper*
150 ml/¼ pint double or whipping cream	*⅔ cup heavy cream*
1 tablespoon French mustard	*1 tablespoon Dijon mustard*
1 tablespoon white wine vinegar	*1 tablespoon white wine vinegar*
good pinch of cumin seeds	*good pinch of cumin seeds*

1. Sprinkle the cabbage or greens with a little salt. Allow to drain for 1 to 2 hours, then dry in a salad spinner or with absorbent kitchen paper.
2. Mix the cabbage or greens, raisins and pepper together in a salad bowl.
3. Place the cream in a bowl with the mustard and stir in the vinegar; do not beat. Leave for a few minutes until the cream begins to thicken.
4. Pour the cream over the cabbage and sprinkle with a few cumin seeds. Toss the salad just before serving.

Dried Fruit Compote

Metric/Imperial	American
500 g/1 lb mixed dried fruit	*3 cups mixed dried fruit*
300 ml/½ pint orange juice	*1¼ cups orange juice*
300 ml/½ pint water	*1¼ cups water*
1 cinnamon stick	*1 cinnamon stick*
2 cloves	*2 cloves*
50 g/2 oz blanched almonds	*½ cup blanched almonds*

1. Put the dried fruit in a bowl and pour over the orange juice and water. Add the spices and leave to soak overnight.
2. Transfer to a pan and bring to the boil.
3. Lower the heat, cover and simmer for about 20 minutes or until the fruit is tender, adding more water if the syrup becomes absorbed. Remove from the heat and set aside. Do not refrigerate.
4. Reheat very gently just before serving. Sprinkle with the almonds and serve warm. ·10·

C · O · U · N · T · D · O · W · N

The day before:
Soak the fruit for the Spiced Fruit Compote.

On the day:
Make the bread. Finish the compote. Prepare salad greens for Spiced Cabbage Salad, wrap in absorbent kitchen paper and chill in a plastic bag. Set table, do flowers. Prepare the mushrooms up to the end of stage 2. Cover with cling film and refrigerate. Prepare the kebabs up to the end of stage 2. Chill the white wine – a good accompaniment would be Verdicchio or Soave. If you choose a light red, such as Beaujolais, you need not open it until you return from the theatre.

To serve at 10 pm:
About 9.15: Preheat the oven (200°C/400°F), Gas Mark 6. Remove the mushrooms from the refrigerator. Serve pre-dinner drinks or cocktails.
About 9.30: Combine all ingredients for the salad and make the dressing.
9.50: Put the mushrooms in the oven to bake. Set kebabs on grill (broiler) rack and season. Brush with oil and set aside. Preheat grill. Warm compote.
10.00: Serve the starter.
Between courses: Pop the kebabs under the grill for 10 minutes, turning occasionally. Toss the salad.

F · R · E · E · Z · E · R · N · O · T · E · S
The Quick Brown Bread will freeze. Cool, wrap and freeze after baking. Thaw overnight.

MENU

· 2 ·

Garden Party for 6

Crudités

·

Black-eye Pea and Fish Salad
New Potatoes with Garlic
Warm Bacon Salad

·

Red Fruit Salad

On lazy summer days, when the grass is freshly mown and the flower beds weeded, there's no better way to celebrate than by entertaining in the garden.

Colour Schemes

Set your prettiest table, if possible choosing crockery and napkins that will echo the colours in your garden. Dark green with cyclamen, perhaps, or shades of yellow to match your roses.

Offer early arrivals iced drinks – sangria or iced tea, depending on their preference and whether or not they still have lawns to mow!

The menu is simple and has been planned to give you, the hostess, as much time as possible to enjoy yourself. Last minute preparation is kept to a minimum.

Indoor Setting

No garden? Don't let that fact deter you. Fill your living room with borrowed potted plants and as many flowers as you can afford, spread a gaily coloured rug on top of your carpet, scatter a few cushions around – and hey presto, you've a garden party no thunderstorm can threaten.

Crudités

Serve a selection of crisp raw vegetables, cut into slim sticks or broken into florets. The recipe below makes a delicious dip. There are a number of variations. Make up several and serve in large or individual containers.

Metric/Imperial	American
1 teaspoon French mustard	1 teaspoon Dijon mustard
150 ml/¼ pint oil	⅔ cup oil
4 tablespoons wine vinegar	4 tablespoons wine vinegar
salt	salt
freshly ground black pepper	freshly ground black pepper
sugar to taste	sugar to taste

1. Combine all the ingredients in a small jar.
2. Cover tightly and shake well to combine thoroughly.
3. Mix again just before serving.

Variations:

Anchovy dressing: Flavour the vinaigrette with a little anchovy essence and garlic.

Ravigote dressing: Add 2 tablespoons finely chopped onion, ½ to 1 tablespoon chopped capers, 1 tablespoon chopped parsley, ½ teaspoon chopped chervil and ½ teaspoon chopped tarragon. ·7·14·

Black-eye Pea and Fish Salad

Metric/Imperial	American
175 g/6 oz black-eye peas	¾ cup black-eye peas
750 ml/1¼ pints water	3 cups water
350 g/12 oz white fish fillets (cod, haddock, etc), cooked, skinned and flaked	¾ lb white fish fillets (cod, haddock, etc), cooked, skinned and flaked
2 × 99 g/3½ oz cans tuna fish, drained and flaked	1 × 6½ oz can tuna fish, drained and flaked
	¾ cup shelled shrimp
175 g/6 oz peeled prawns	1 medium onion, grated
1 medium onion, grated	⅔ cup Vinaigrette Dressing (see Crudités)
150 ml/¼ pint Vinaigrette Dressing (see Crudités)	finely grated rind and juice of ½ lemon
finely grated rind and juice of ½ lemon	dash of hot pepper sauce
dash of Tabasco sauce	2 teaspoons tomato paste
2 teaspoons tomato purée	2 tablespoons chopped parsley
2 tablespoons chopped parsley	salt
salt	freshly ground black pepper
freshly ground black pepper	For Garnish:
To Garnish:	few shrimp, in shells
few unpeeled prawns	parsley sprigs
parsley sprigs	

1. Put the peas in a large bowl, cover with the water, then leave to soak overnight. Alternatively, pour over boiling water and soak for several hours.
2. Transfer the peas and water to a pan and bring to the boil. Lower the heat, cover and simmer for 1 to 1½ hours until the peas are tender, adding more water if necessary.
3. Drain the peas and place in a bowl. Add the flaked fish and prawns (shrimp) and fold lightly to mix.
4. Mix together the remaining ingredients, then fold into the salad. Leave to marinate for at least 1 hour.
5. Turn onto a serving dish, garnish with the prawns and parsley, and serve cold.

New Potatoes with Garlic

Metric/Imperial	American
1 kg/2 lb new potatoes	2 lb new potatoes
salt	salt
1 clove garlic, peeled and crushed	1 clove garlic, peeled and crushed
75 g/3 oz softened butter	⅓ cup softened butter
1 tablespoon chopped parsley	1 tablespoon chopped parsley

Crudités and vinaigrette

1. Scrub the potatoes but do not skin them.
2. Bring a saucepan of salted water to the boil, add the potatoes and cook for 15 to 20 minutes until just tender.
3. Remove from the heat, drain off the water and place a clean folded tea towel on top of the potatoes. Replace the pan lid. This will keep the potatoes warm while drawing out any excess moisture.
4. Meanwhile, combine the garlic with the butter.
5. When ready to serve, toss the potatoes in the garlic butter and garnish with parsley. ·8·

Variation:

Beat 25 g/1 oz grated Cheddar cheese plus a pinch of dried tarragon into 75 g/3 oz softened butter. Stir into the hot potatoes and serve.

Warm Bacon Salad

Metric/Imperial	American
1 large lettuce	1 large head lettuce
50 g/2 oz bacon, diced	2 slices bacon, diced
Dressing:	Dressing:
juice of 1 lemon	juice of 1 lemon
1 tablespoon finely chopped parsley	1 tablespoon finely chopped parsley
pinch of sugar	pinch of sugar
salt	salt
freshly ground black pepper	freshly ground black pepper

1. Separate the lettuce into leaves and tear roughly. Wash and dry the leaves and wrap loosely in absorbent kitchen paper. Place in the refrigerator for 1 or 2 hours to crisp.

11

2. Combine the ingredients for the dressing in a small jar. Cover tightly and shake until thoroughly combined.

3. Just before serving, fry the bacon in its own fat in a small frying pan (skillet) until crisp and golden.

4. Place the lettuce leaves in a salad bowl, toss with enough dressing to moisten lightly and sprinkle over the hot bacon. Serve immediately. ·12·

Red Fruit Salad

Metric/Imperial	American
450 ml/3/4 pint water	2 cups water
175 g/6 oz caster sugar	3/4 cup superfine sugar
250 g/8 oz fresh redcurrants, stalks removed	2 cups fresh red currants, stems removed
500 g/1 lb strawberries, hulled	3 cups strawberries, hulled
250 g/8 oz raspberries	1½ cups raspberries

1. Place the water and sugar in a pan and heat gently to dissolve the sugar, then boil for 3 minutes. Remove from the heat and allow to cool for 5 minutes.

2. Stir in the redcurrants and leave until quite cold.

3. Add the strawberries and raspberries. Spoon into a bowl and chill.

4. Serve with cream. ·12·

C · O · U · N · T · D · O · W · N

Two days before:
Prepare the black-eye peas for the Fish Salad. Cover with water and leave to soak overnight.

The day before:
Make the dressings. At the same time make the dressing for the Warm Bacon Salad. Cover each with cling film (plastic wrap) and store in a cool place. Cook the black-eye peas, drain, and cool. Store, covered, in the refrigerator. Make a big jug of sangria or iced tea (or both). Chill, covered, in the refrigerator. Cook the fish for the main salad and transfer with a slotted spoon to a china dish. Cover tightly and refrigerate. Make the garlic butter for the new potatoes and chill. Make the Red Fruit Salad. Cover and chill.

On the day:
Prepare the Crudités, arranging them attractively on one or two large platters or on individual plates. Cover with cling film and chill. Wash and dry the greens for the Warm Bacon Salad and place, lightly wrapped in absorbent kitchen paper, in the crisper of the refrigerator. Chop parsley for garnishing and set aside parsley sprigs for the fish salad. Shell the prawns (shrimp) and flake the tuna. Finish making the dressing for the fish salad. Decant dressings. Chill white wine, if serving.

To serve at 1 pm:
About 11: Mix together all the ingredients for the Black-eye Pea and Fish Salad, cover and leave to marinate.

About noon: Arrange the fish salad on a large platter, garnish with prawns and parsley and return, covered, to the refrigerator.

About 12.30: Whip cream, if using, to soft peaks, sweeten lightly and place in the refrigerator until required for the fruit salad. Remove the garlic butter from the refrigerator.

12.40: Put the potatoes on to boil.

1.00: Drain potatoes, cover with clean cloth. If serving wines, take them to the garden. Serve Crudités and dressings.

Between courses: Fry the bacon. Toss the potatoes in garlic butter and sprinkle with parsley. Toss the green salad and sprinkle with the hot bacon. Serve the fish salad, with Red Fruit Salad and cream to follow.

F · R · E · E · Z · E · R · N · O · T · E · S
Only the Red Fruit Salad will freeze. Pack and freeze at the end of stage 3. Thaw overnight in the refrigerator.

· 3 ·

High Fibre Brunch Party for 6

Swiss Breakfast
Muesli

·

Pipérade

·

Lemon Breakfast Muffins
Yogurt Wholemeal Scones

Have you ever had a brunch party? They're great fun.

Guests arrive about 10 am; dress is casual and the aim is to create as relaxed an atmosphere as possible – the antidote to work-a-day breakfasts, when everyone is in a hurry and conversation is limited to monosyllables.

Everyone does his own thing. If some of your guests want to go for a jog around the park or play squash before nosh, let them. But don't neglect the torpid types. Supply a stack of Sunday papers, a selection of records, perhaps even a board game or two.

Get the party off to a good start by serving Bucks Fizz – champagne and orange juice, or Black Velvet – champagne and Guinness.

High Fibre Feast

We've devised a breakfast with some luxury touches. To start, there's a choice of Muesli or Swiss Breakfast – a blend of oats, fruit, nuts and cream. Swiss Breakfast is best made to order as it will not keep, so determine your guests' tastes in advance and make up individual portions.

Muffins and wholewheat scones, served in linen-lined baskets, make a fine finale. Serve with butter and a selection of spreads, including honey, homemade jams and marmalade.

Swiss Breakfast

Metric/Imperial	American
1 tablespoon wheatgerm	*1 tablespoon wheatgerm*
1 tablespoon rolled oats	*1 tablespoon rolled oats*
4 tablespoons water	*¼ cup water*
1 teaspoon lemon juice	*1 teaspoon lemon juice*
1 teaspoon orange juice	*1 teaspoon orange juice*
1 eating apple	*1 dessert apple*
1 tablespoon clear honey	*1 tablespoon runny honey*
2 tablespoon single cream	*2 tablespoons light cream*
25 g/1 oz hazelnuts, chopped	*¼ cup chopped hazelnuts*

To Serve:
*fresh fruit in season
(bananas, grapes,
peaches, raspberries,
strawberries, etc)*

To Serve:
*fresh fruit in season
(bananas, grapes,
peaches, raspberries,
strawberries, etc)*

1. Put the wheatgerm, oats and water in a serving bowl. Cover and leave in the refrigerator overnight.
2. The next morning, stir in the lemon and orange juice. Do not peel the apple but grate it, then stir into the oat mixture with the honey and cream.
3. Sprinkle on the nuts and serve immediately, with fresh fruit in season.

Muesli

Metric/Imperial	American
250 g/8 oz rolled oats	2¼ cups rolled oats
250 g/8 oz barley flakes or kernels, sesame and sunflower seeds, bran and wheatgerm, mixed according to taste	2¼ cups barley flakes or kernels, sesame and sunflower seeds, bran and wheatgerm, mixed according to taste
50 g/2 oz mixed nuts, chopped	½ cup mixed chopped nuts
50 g/2 oz seedless raisins and coarsely chopped dried fruit (apples, apricots, dates, figs), mixed according to taste	⅓ cup seedless raisins and coarsely chopped dried fruit (apples, apricots, dates, figs), mixed according to taste

1. Put the oats in a bowl, then stir in the remaining ingredients.
2. Store in an airtight container and use as required.
3. Serve with brown sugar or honey and milk, cream or yogurt. Fresh fruit may be added according to season.

Pipérade

Metric/Imperial	American
3 tablespoons oil	3 tablespoons oil
1½ onions, thinly sliced	1½ onions, thinly sliced
2 large green peppers, cored, seeded and sliced	2 large green peppers, seeded and sliced
2 cloves garlic, peeled and crushed	2 cloves garlic, peeled and crushed
350 g/12 oz tomatoes, skinned and chopped	¾ lb tomatoes, peeled and chopped
salt	salt
freshly ground black pepper	freshly ground black pepper
9 eggs	9 eggs
6 rashers bacon (optional)	6 bacon slices (optional)

Swiss breakfast and Muesli.

1. Heat the oil in a large frying pan (skillet) and sauté the onion until soft. Add the peppers and garlic and continue to cook for 5 minutes. Add the tomatoes and salt and pepper to taste; cover and cook for 20 minutes.
2. Lightly beat the eggs, pour into the vegetables and stir continuously until the eggs are just set.
3. While cooking the eggs, place the bacon under a preheated moderate grill (broiler) so that it is cooked when the eggs are ready.
4. Spoon the pipérade onto a warm, flat serving dish and arrange the bacon on top, if liked. Omit the bacon if vegetarians are to be served.

Lemon Breakfast Muffins

Metric/Imperial	American
25 g/1 oz All Bran breakfast cereal	½ cup All Bran breakfast cereal
5 tablespoons milk	⅓ cup milk
25 g/1 oz butter	2 tablespoons butter
25 g/1 oz soft brown sugar	2 tablespoons light brown sugar
1 egg, beaten	1 egg, beaten
1 tablespoon chopped walnuts	1 tablespoon chopped walnuts
2 tablespoons lemon curd	2 tablespoons lemon cheese
50 g/2 oz wholemeal flour	½ cup wholewheat flour
1½ teaspoons baking powder	1½ teaspoons baking powder

1. Place the breakfast cereal in a bowl with the milk and leave until soft.
2. Add the butter, sugar, egg, nuts and lemon curd (cheese) and beat until the mixture is smooth.
3. Sift together the flour and baking powder and gently fold into the milk mixture. Do not overmix.
4. Spoon the mixture into six greased deep bun tins (muffin pans) and bake in a preheated oven (200°C/400°F), Gas Mark 6 for 20 minutes or until golden and springy to touch. Serve warm. Makes 6.

Yogurt Wholemeal Scones

Metric/Imperial	American
250 g/8 oz wholemeal flour	2 cups wholewheat flour
1/2 teaspoon salt	1/2 teaspoon salt
1 1/2 teaspoons baking powder	1 1/2 teaspoons baking powder
25 g/1 oz vegetable margarine	2 tablespoons vegetable margarine
150 ml/1/4 pint natural yogurt	2/3 cup unflavored yogurt

1. Put the flour, salt and baking powder in a bowl and stir well to mix. Rub (cut) in the margarine, then stir in the yogurt and mix to a soft dough.
2. Turn out onto a lightly floured surface and knead lightly for 30 seconds. Roll out to 2 cm/3/4 inch thickness, cut out ten rounds with a 5 cm (2 inch) biscuit (cookie) cutter and place on a greased baking sheet.
3. Bake in a preheated oven (200°C/400°F), Gas Mark 6 for 12 minutes. Transfer to a wire rack and leave to cool. Makes 10.

C · O · U · N · T · D · O · W · N

The day before:
Find out how many of your guests would like the Swiss Breakfast, and start to prepare individual servings. Place wheatgerm, oats and water in each serving bowl, cover and leave in the refrigerator overnight. Make the Muesli base.

On the day:
Collect the Sunday papers. Prepare and chill individual bowls of fresh fruit – bananas, grapes, peaches, raspberries, strawberries etc, to accompany the Swiss Breakfast or Muesli or to be offered as a third choice. Squeeze oranges for Bucks Fizz. Prepare the vegetables for the Pipérade. Bake scones and leave to cool on wire racks. To keep them soft, cover them lightly with clean tea towels. Prepare the muffin mixture up to the end of stage 2. Lay the table and set the scene. Remember that the accent is on comfort, so make sure your living and dining areas are pleasantly warm. If it is winter, an open fire is lovely, but don't build it up too high. You want your guests relaxed, but not comatose!

As guests arrive:
Serve Bucks Fizz or Black Velvet (or plain fruit juice if preferred).

To serve at 11.30 am:
10.30: Preheat the oven.
10.50: Finish making the muffin batter.
11.00: Bake the muffins. Prepare the Pipérade up to the end of stage 1.
11.15: Complete the individual Swiss Breakfasts. Set out the Muesli, with brown sugar or honey and milk, cream or yogurt. Arrange bowls of chilled fresh fruit on the table.
11.25: Remove the muffins from the oven and cool slightly on wire racks. Preheat the grill (broiler).
11.30: Serve breakfast. While your guests are enjoying the first course, complete the Pipérade and set out the scones and muffins, together with butter, honey, marmalade, and a selection of homemade jams. Make coffee, if serving.

F · R · E · E · Z · E · R · N · O · T · E · S

Cool, pack and freeze the Lemon Breakfast Muffins and Yogurt Wholemeal Scones after baking. Thaw overnight at cool room temperature. Refresh in a hot oven for 10 to 15 minutes before serving.

Cook's Tip:
A warm fruit compote is always welcome at breakfast time, especially on chilly winter mornings. Use our recipe on page 8 for the basic quantities, then experiment with your own combinations of fruit and spices. The compote can be warmed through in the oven. Spoon the mixture into a shallow casserole, cover tightly, and place in the bottom of a moderate oven for 15 to 20 minutes. Sprinkle the warmed compote with a few toasted sesame or pumpkin seeds before serving.

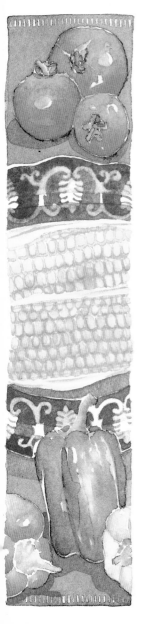

~M·E·N·U~

· 4 ·

Pizza Picnic for 4

Watercress Soup
·
Wholemeal Pizza
Lettuce and Orange Salad
·
Fruity Yogurt
Oatmeal Crunchies

Pizza is the perfect picnic food. Ours has a high-fibre wholemeal base and a generous topping that's packed with goodness – a blend of bacon, ham, spinach, tomatoes and cheese, it is virtually a meal on the move.

To precede the pizza, there is Watercress Soup, fresh and cleansing to the palate and, to accompany it, Lettuce and Orange Salad.

We suggest you close the proceedings with a fruity yogurt dessert, served with crunchy oatmeal biscuits (cookies).

It all adds up to a wonderful repast, and one that's as healthy and invigorating as the country air itself.

On the Move

All the food is easily prepared and transported, so you can concentrate on the accessories. Old-fashioned hampers look the part and are ideal for carrying cutlery and crockery, but a cool box is best for transporting the food. If you have picnic table and chairs you can dine in style, but you could be just as comfortable propped on cushions on a picnic rug.

The choice of crockery is up to you, but if you're buying a picnic set, look out for the new, brightly coloured enamel plates and mugs. There are some super plastics available, too.

Watercress Soup

Metric/Imperial	American
2 bunches watercress, trimmed	2 bunches watercress, trimmed
1 tablespoon oil	1 tablespoon oil
1 small onion, finely chopped	1 small onion, finely chopped
600 ml/1 pint chicken or vegetable stock	2½ cups chicken or vegetable stock
2 egg yolks	2 egg yolks
150 ml/¼ pint natural yogurt	⅔ cup unflavored yogurt
salt	salt
freshly ground white pepper	freshly ground white pepper

1. Chop the watercress and stems.
2. Heat the oil in a pan, add the onion and sauté gently until soft and golden. Add the watercress and the stock and bring to the boil. Lower the heat, cover and simmer for 20 minutes.
3. Rub the soup through a sieve (strainer), or work to a purée in a blender or food processor.
4. Put the egg yolks in a bowl and whisk in the yogurt. Stir in 4 tablespoons (¼ cup) of the purée and mix well.
5. Pour the remaining purée into the rinsed-out pan. Add the yogurt mixture, stirring constantly, then heat through gently without boiling. Taste for seasoning. Serve chilled. ·5·9·

Wholemeal Pizza

Metric/Imperial	American
Base:	Base:
15 g/½ oz fresh yeast or 1½ teaspoons dried yeast and ½ teaspoon sugar	½ cake compressed yeast or 1½ teaspoons active dry yeast and ½ teaspoon sugar
6-7 tablespoons warm milk	6-7 tablespoons warm milk
250 g/8 oz wholemeal flour	2 cups wholewheat flour
salt	

freshly ground black pepper	salt
25 g/1 oz butter	freshly ground black pepper
Topping:	2 tablespoons butter
1 tablespoon olive oil	Topping:
1 onion, chopped	1 tablespoon olive oil
2 rashers streaky bacon, chopped	1 onion, chopped
75 g/3 oz cooked ham, chopped	2 bacon slices, chopped
500 g/1 lb fresh spinach	⅓ cup chopped cooked ham
pinch of nutmeg	1 lb fresh spinach
garlic salt	pinch of nutmeg
½ teaspoon lemon juice	garlic salt
250 g/8 oz tomatoes, sliced	½ teaspoon lemon juice
125 g/4 oz mozzarella cheese, sliced	½ lb tomatoes, sliced
¼ teaspoon dried oregano	¼ lb mozzarella cheese, sliced
	¼ teaspoon dried oregano

1. Blend the fresh yeast in the warm milk, or dissolve the sugar in the warm milk and sprinkle the dried yeast on top. Leave the yeast in a warm place for 10 minutes until frothy.
2. Mix the flour, salt and pepper together then rub (cut) in the butter. Make a well in the centre and pour in the yeast mixture. Stir well until the mixture forms a ball. Knead on a lightly floured surface for 5 minutes. Place dough in an oiled polythene (plastic) bag and leave in a warm place for 1 hour until doubled in size.
3. Meanwhile heat the oil in a small saucepan and sauté the onion and bacon for 5 minutes until the onion is soft. Add the cooked ham. Cool.
4. Wash the spinach and cook in the water clinging to the leaves in a covered pan for 3 minutes. Season with nutmeg, garlic salt and lemon juice. Drain thoroughly and cool.
5. Turn the dough onto a lightly floured board and knead again for 1 minute. Roll out to a 28 cm/11 inch round and place on an oiled baking sheet.
6. Cover the base with the spinach and bacon, onion and ham. Top with the sliced tomatoes and cheese

and sprinkle over the oregano.

7. Place in a preheated oven (200°C/400°F), Gas Mark 6 and bake for 25 minutes. Serve cold, cut into wedges. ·9·

Lettuce and Orange Salad

Metric/Imperial	American
1 crisp lettuce	*1 head crisp lettuce*
2 oranges	*2 oranges*
4 tablespoons olive oil or walnut oil	*¼ cup olive oil or walnut oil*
50 g/2 oz blanched almonds, cut into slivers	*½ cup blanched almonds, cut into slivers*
1 tablespoon lemon juice or orange juice	*1 tablespoon lemon juice or orange juice*
salt	*salt*
freshly ground black pepper	*freshly ground black pepper*

Wholemeal pizza

1. Wash and dry the lettuce, tear it into pieces and wrap it loosely in absorbent kitchen paper. Store in the refrigerator until required.

2. Remove the peel and pith from the oranges and cut the flesh into segments between the membranes, working over a bowl so that all juice is saved. Store segments and juice in a sealed container in the refrigerator until needed.

3. Heat the oil and sauté the almonds, stirring constantly for about 3 minutes.

4. Allow the almonds to cool, then stir the lemon juice, salt and pepper into the pan. Store the dressing in an airtight jar.

5. When ready to serve, combine the lettuce and the orange segments, with their juice, in a salad bowl. Pour over the dressing and toss well. ·11·

Fruity Yogurt

Metric/Imperial	American
2 tablespoons soft brown sugar	2 tablespoons light brown sugar
150 ml/¼ pint natural yogurt	⅔ cup unflavored yogurt
2 tablespoons mixed dried fruits (sultanas, raisins, chopped dates)	2 tablespoons mixed dried fruits (golden raisins, raisins, chopped dates)
1 tablespoon chopped candied peel	1 tablespoon chopped candied peel
2 tablespoons chopped hazelnuts	2 tablespoons chopped hazelnuts
1 large banana, peeled and chopped	1 large banana, peeled and chopped

1. Gently fold the brown sugar into the yogurt. Stir until well blended.
2. Fold in the dried fruits and most of the nuts, reserving a few to decorate. Toss the banana in the lemon juice and lastly fold this into the mixture.
3. Divide the dessert carefully between four plastic serving dishes and decorate each one with a sprinkling of the reserved nuts. Cover with airtight lids, seal and chill until required.

Cook's Tip:
Flavoured yogurts give delicious results, too. Hazelnut and peach are especially good.

Oatmeal Crunchies

Metric/Imperial	American
125 g/4 oz wholemeal flour	1 cup wholewheat flour
50 g/2 oz oatmeal	⅓ cup oatmeal
25 g/1 oz bran	½ cup bran
50 g/2 oz muscovado sugar	⅓ cup, packed, Barbados sugar
¼ teaspoon ground ginger	¼ teaspoon ground ginger
¼ teaspoon ground mixed spice	¼ teaspoon ground apple pie spice
50 g/2 oz vegetable	

margarine	¼ cup vegetable margarine
120 ml/4 fl oz cold water (approximately)	½ cup cold water (approximately)

1. Put the dry ingredients in a bowl and mix well.
2. Rub (cut) in the margarine until the mixture resembles coarse breadcrumbs, then add enough water to make a stiff dough.
3. Turn out onto a lightly floured surface, then roll out to 1 cm/½ inch thickness. Cut out 24 rounds with a 5 cm/2 inch biscuit (cookie) cutter.
4. Place on greased baking sheets, then bake in a preheated oven (180°C/350°F), Gas Mark 4 for 25 minutes. Transfer to a wire rack and leave to cool.
·11·

C · O · U · N · T · D · O · W · N
We assume you set off for your picnic about 10.30 am and have therefore scheduled quite a lot of preparation for the last minute. If you plan an evening picnic or wish to set off at crack of dawn, you'll need to adjust the timing.

The day before:
Bake the crunchies, cool on wire racks, then pack neatly into an airtight container. Prepare the watercress soup up to the end of stage 3. Cool, transfer to a deep bowl and cover with cling film (plastic wrap). Store in the refrigerator. Make the pizza. When cold, wrap tightly in foil and store in the refrigerator.

On the day:
Finish the soup. Chill for as long as possible before your departure. Chill the wine. Take chilled soda (carbonated) water, too, as some guests may prefer a spritzer. Wash and dry lettuce and pack it into a plastic box. Segment oranges and pack separately. Finally make the dressing and carry it in a well sealed jar. Make the yogurt and fruit dessert and divide it between four bowls with airtight seals. Store in the refrigerator. Transfer the soup to a chilled, wide-mouthed vacuum flask. Pack cutlery, plates and food into a hamper and go!

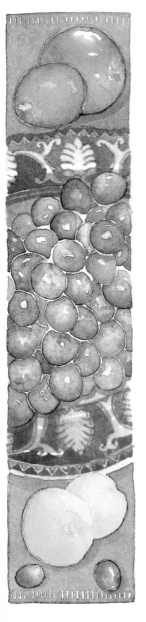

MENU

· 5 ·

Vegetarian Feast for 4

Green Garden Soup

·

Nut Roast
Carrot Purée
Peas à la Française

·

Citrus Pancakes

A Feast from the Garden

Everything in the garden is lovely and is used to good effect in this beautifully balanced meal. It's a treat for the eyes as well as the palate and you don't have to be a vegetarian to enjoy it. Make it for the family, as a change from the traditional Sunday lunch.

It often happens that just one of your guests is a vegetarian, which can put you in a quandary. Invariably the vegetarian will insist you don't make a fuss on her behalf. 'I'll be quite happy with salad or vegetables and perhaps a piece of cheese.' As a hostess, however, you want to create a menu that will please everyone. Here it is. The Nut Roast is hearty enough to satisfy the most ardent carnivore and the structure of the meal is still fairly traditional, with three courses as opposed to the more relaxed vegetarian meal where several courses of equal emphasis may be served.

The Nut Roast is an excellent source of protein and fat – a fine energy-booster. The nuts also provide dietary fibre (over 6 grams per serving). The vegetables supply vitamins and minerals and additional fibre – the peas are a particularly good source. Serve the soup with wholemeal (wholewheat) rolls and you'll have created a meal that's as nutritionally sound as you can make it.

Green Garden Soup

Metric/Imperial	American
4 celery sticks, chopped	4 celery stalks, chopped
2 leeks, shredded	2 leeks, shredded
1 bunch of watercress, stalks trimmed	1 bunch of watercress, stems trimmed
3 courgettes, thinly sliced	3 zucchini, thinly sliced
600 ml/1 pint vegetable stock	2½ cups vegetable stock
salt	salt
freshly ground black pepper	freshly ground black pepper
1 clove garlic, peeled and crushed	1 clove garlic, peeled and crushed
1 small bunch of parsley	1 small bunch of parsley
150 ml/¼ pint natural yogurt	⅔ cup unflavored yogurt
chopped fresh chives, to garnish	chopped fresh chives, for garnish

1. Put the celery, leeks, watercress and courgettes (zucchini) into a saucepan together with the vegetable stock, salt and pepper to taste, garlic and parsley. Simmer gently until the vegetables are just tender – about 15 minutes.
2. Purée in a blender or food processor until smooth. Cool, then stir in half the yogurt. Chill.
3. Serve in chilled soup bowls with a little of the remaining yogurt swirled on top. Garnish with chopped chives. ·1·4·

Nut Roast

Metric/Imperial	American
50 g/2 oz vegetarian fat or margarine	¼ cup vegetarian fat or margarine
2 medium onions, chopped	2 medium onions, chopped
1 clove garlic, peeled and chopped	1 clove garlic, peeled and chopped
1 small dessert apple, peeled and chopped	1 small eating apple, pared and chopped
350 g/12 oz peanuts or cashew nuts or other nuts	1½ cups peanuts or 3 cups cashew nuts or other nuts
1 teaspoon chopped fresh sage or ½ teaspoon dried sage	1 teaspoon chopped fresh sage or ½ teaspoon dried sage
50 g/2 oz fresh wholemeal breadcrumbs	1 cup soft wholewheat bread crumbs
2 eggs	2 eggs
4 tablespoons milk	¼ cup milk
salt and pepper	salt and pepper
2 tomatoes, sliced, to garnish	2 sliced tomatoes, to garnish

1. Heat the fat or margarine in a large saucepan and sauté the onions, garlic and apple until soft.
2. Grind the nuts in a nut mill or chop in a food processor and add to the onion mixture, together with the sage, breadcrumbs, eggs and milk.
3. Season well and place in a greased 1.2 litre/2 pint (1 quart) pie dish or loaf pan.
4. Bake in the centre of a preheated oven (180°C/350°F), Gas Mark 4, for 35 to 40 minutes. Serve hot. ·9·

Cook's Tip:
If you bake the nut roast in a loaf tin, grease the tin well and coat with toasted wholemeal breadcrumbs before adding the mixture. This not only gives the loaf an attractive appearance, but also helps you turn it out.

Carrot Purée

Metric/Imperial	American
1 kg/2 lb carrots, diced	5 cups diced carrots
150 ml/¼ pint vegetable stock	⅔ cup vegetable stock
75 g/3 oz butter	6 tablespoons butter
salt	salt
freshly ground black pepper	freshly ground black pepper
3 tablespoons natural yogurt, to serve	3 tablespoons unflavored yogurt, to serve

1. Put the carrots and stock into a pan and bring to the boil. Lower the heat, cover tightly with a lid and simmer for 10 to 15 minutes, until the carrots are very tender.

2. Remove the lid, increase the heat and boil rapidly for 2 to 3 minutes, until most of the liquid has evaporated.

3. Remove from the heat and stir in the butter. Cool slightly, then work the carrots in a blender or food processor until smooth. Season with salt and pepper to taste.

4. Reheat if necessary, and stir in the yogurt to serve. ·6·

Peas à la Française

Metric/Imperial
500 g/1 lb shelled fresh
  peas
1 bunch of spring onions,
  trimmed and chopped

American
1 lb hulled fresh peas
1 bunch of scallions,
  trimmed and chopped
¼ cup butter

50 g/2 oz butter
1 teaspoon brown sugar
salt
freshly ground black pepper
4 tablespoons water
1 crisp lettuce

1 teaspoon brown sugar
salt
freshly ground black pepper
¼ cup water
1 crisp head lettuce

1. Place the peas in a heavy-based pan with the spring onions (scallions), half of the butter, the sugar, salt and pepper to taste, and the water. Bring to the boil, cover and simmer for 10 minutes.

2. Remove the outer leaves of the lettuce and discard. Cut the heart into quarters and add to the pan. Cover the pan and simmer for a further 3 to 5 minutes, shaking the pan occasionally to turn over the contents.

3. Remove from the heat, add the remaining butter and toss well. Transfer to a warmed serving dish and serve immediately.

Citrus pancakes

Citrus Pancakes

Metric/Imperial	American
For the Pancakes:	For the Pancakes:
125 g/4 oz wholemeal flour	1 cup wholewheat flour
1 teaspoon grated lemon rind	1 teaspoon grated lemon rind
pinch of salt	pinch of salt
1 egg	1 egg
150 ml/¼ pint milk	⅔ cup milk
150 ml/¼ pint water	⅔ cup water
1 tablespoon melted butter	1 tablespoon melted butter
oil for frying	oil for frying
For the Filling:	For the Filling:
50 g/2 oz butter	¼ cup butter
50 g/2 oz soft brown sugar	⅓ cup, packed, light brown sugar
1 teaspoon grated lemon rind	1 teaspoon grated lemon rind
1 teaspoon grated orange rind	1 teaspoon grated orange rind
1 tablespoon lemon juice	1 tablespoon lemon juice
2 tablespoons orange juice	2 tablespoons orange juice
lemon and orange slices (optional), to decorate	lemon and orange slices (optional), to decorate

1. For the pancakes, sift the flour and salt into a bowl. Add the lemon rind, egg, milk and water. Gradually incorporate the flour into the egg and milk mixture, beating well until a smooth batter forms. Cover and leave at cool room temperature for 30 minutes.

2. Stir in the melted butter and use the batter to make eight pancakes, frying them in a little oil.

3. To make the filling, cream together the butter, sugar and grated fruit rinds, then gradually beat in the fruit juices. Do this very slowly to avoid curdling the mixture.

4. To serve, spread each pancake with a little of the butter mixture and fold into four. Decorate with the citrus slices if wished. ·1·

The day before:
Prepare the Green Garden Soup to the end of stage 2. Cover with cling film (plastic wrap) and chill. Make the pancakes.

On the day:
Make the Nut Roast mixture. Store in refrigerator. Prepare the vegetables for the Peas à la Française: Cut the heart of the lettuce into quarters, wash and dry it and place in the refrigerator, loosely wrapped in absorbent kitchen paper. Make the citrus butter for the pancakes and chill. Set the table, do the flowers, make butter curls for serving with the rolls. Set out the wines. With the Nut Roast, serve a vigorous red wine such as Chianti or Zinfandel.

To serve at 8 pm:
6.00: Open the red wine and decant if desired.
7.20: Preheat oven to (180°C/350°F), Gas Mark 4.
7.30: Make the Carrot Purée to the end of stage 3.
7.40: Bake the Nut Roast. Remove the citrus butter from the refrigerator and allow to come to room temperature.
7.45: Pour soup into individual chilled bowls, swirl yogurt on top and garnish with chives.
8.00: Wrap pancakes in foil and pop into the oven to heat through. Put the peas on to boil, then leave, barely simmering, while you serve the soup and rolls. *Between courses:* Turn out the roast if baked in loaf tin (pan) and decorate with tomato slices. Reheat the Carrot Purée, and stir in yogurt. Finish cooking the peas with the lettuce. Finally spread the pancakes with citrus butter, fold and serve.

F · R · E · E · Z · E · R · N · O · T · E · S

Cool, pack and freeze the Carrot Purée without the yogurt. Thaw overnight in the refrigerator. Reheat gently in a saucepan with a little extra butter. Stir in the yogurt as per recipe. Cool, pack and freeze the pancakes. Thaw overnight at cool room temperature. Wrap and freeze the citrus butter. Thaw overnight in the refrigerator. Finish as per recipe.

MENU

· 6 ·

Family Supper for 4

Watercress with Orange and Nuts

·

Crispy-coated Liver
Jacket Potatoes with Yogurt and Chives

·

Creamy Apple Flan

Sometimes it's difficult to feed your family the food you know is good for them. Children go to birthday parties and fill up on crisps, biscuits (cookies) and fizzy drinks; working husbands (wives, too) grab wildly unsuitable snacks from the office tea-trolley or over-indulge at restaurant or pub.

Healthy Eating

Redress the balance with this nutritious menu. The main course is built around liver, which is an excellent food. The quantity in our recipe will provide every member of the family with almost half his or her daily recommended intake of protein, plus enough iron, vitamin A and vitamin B2 for two days. It also contains vitamins C and D. Additional vitamins are provided by the vegetables and fruit and there's a generous contribution to the day's dietary fibre requirements.

A Family Affair

There's quite a bit of last-minute preparation, which is why we've made this a meal for the family rather than a menu for a dinner party. However, if you have the kind of friends who like to keep you company while you cook (or, better still, help), by all means offer them this meal.

Watercress with Orange and Nuts

Metric/Imperial	American
1 bunch of watercress	1 bunch of watercress
1 large orange	1 large orange
2 tablespoons chopped hazelnuts	2 tablespoons chopped hazelnuts
Dressing:	Dressing:
120 ml/4 fl oz natural yogurt	1/2 cup unflavored yogurt
1 clove garlic, peeled and crushed	1 clove garlic, peeled and crushed
pinch of sugar	pinch of sugar
2 teaspoons chopped parsley	2 teaspoons chopped parsley
freshly ground black pepper	freshly ground black pepper

1. Trim the watercress, place in a sieve (strainer), rinse and drain thoroughly. Place in a large serving bowl.
2. Remove the peel and pith from the orange, and cut the flesh into segments between the membranes. Chop segments roughly.
3. Add the orange and hazelnuts to the watercress.
4. Make the dressing. Beat the yogurt with the garlic, sugar, parsley and pepper to taste.
5. Pour over the watercress and toss well. Leave to stand for about 30 minutes at room temperature before serving, to allow the flavours to develop. ·1·10·

Cook's Tip:
For special occasions, serve individual portions in grapefruit or orange shells.

Crispy-coated Liver

Metric/Imperial	American
75 g/3 oz butter	6 tablespoons butter
1 large onion, sliced into rings	1 large onion, sliced into rings
25 g/1 oz plain flour	1/4 cup all-purpose flour
salt	salt
freshly ground black pepper	freshly ground black pepper
1/2 teaspoon dried mixed herbs	1/2 teaspoon dried mixed herbs
1 egg	1 egg
1 tablespoon milk	1 tablespoon milk
500 g/1 lb lambs' liver, thinly sliced diagonally	1 lb lambs' liver, thinly sliced diagonally
50 g/2 oz rolled porridge oats	1/2 cup rolled porridge oats
120 ml/4 fl oz medium sherry	1/2 cup medium sherry
120 ml/4 fl oz chicken stock	1/2 cup chicken stock
sprigs of parsley, to garnish	sprigs of parsley, for garnish

1. Melt 25 g/1 oz (2 tablespoons) of the butter in a frying pan (skillet) and sauté the onion rings over moderate heat for 5 to 6 minutes, turning occasionally. Remove the onion rings from the pan and keep warm.
2. Mix the flour with the salt and pepper and stir in the dried herbs. Beat the egg and milk together. Dry the liver slices on absorbent kitchen paper. Dip them first into the seasoned flour, then into the milk mixture and finally into the oats. Press the oats on firmly to make an even coating.
3. Melt the remaining butter in the pan. When hot, cook the liver slices over moderate heat for about 3 minutes on each side, until the coating is crisp and brown. The liver should still be pink inside (test it by piercing with a sharp knife).
4. Remove the liver from the pan and keep it warm. Tip in any remaining seasoned flour and stir well. Pour on the sherry and stock and bring to the boil, adding salt and pepper to taste and stirring until thickened.
5. Arrange the liver on a heated platter, scatter the onion rings on top and pour over the sauce. Garnish with sprigs of parsley. ·5·10·

Jacket Potatoes with Yogurt and Chives

Metric/Imperial	American
4 large potatoes, scrubbed but not peeled	*4 large potatoes, scrubbed but not peeled*
salt to taste	*salt to taste*
120 ml/4 fl oz natural yogurt	*½ cup unflavored yogurt*
4 tablespoons chopped chives	*4 tablespoons chopped chives*

1. Bake the potatoes in their jackets in a preheated oven (190-200°C/375-400°F), Gas Mark 5-6 for about 1 hour or until cooked.
2. Stand the potatoes on a serving dish and cut a large cross in the top of each one. Then, using a cloth to protect your hands, squeeze the base of each potato until each top opens out. Season with salt and pepper to taste.
3. Spoon 2 tablespoons yogurt into each potato and top with 1 tablespoon chopped chives. Serve immediately. ·8·

Cook's Tip:
If you have a microwave oven, cooking the potatoes is child's play. Scrub them as usual, prick each potato several times and wrap them in absorbent kitchen paper. Cook for 12 to 15 minutes on full power.

If you are serving Crispy-coated Liver to small children, you may prefer to omit the sherry and increase the chicken stock to 240 ml/8 fl oz (1 cup). Alternatively replace the liver with strips of skinless chicken or turkey breast fillets and cook for about 5 to 7 minutes on each side or until cooked through.

Watercress with orange and nuts

Creamy Apple Flan

Metric/Imperial	American
Rich Wholemeal Pastry	**Rich Wholewheat Pastry**
125 g/4 oz wholemeal flour	*1 cup wholewheat flour*
pinch of salt	*pinch of salt*
50 g/2 oz butter, cut into small pieces	*1/4 cup butter, cut into small pieces*
1 egg yolk	*1 egg yolk*
2 tablespoons soft brown sugar	*2 tablespoons light brown sugar*
1-2 tablespoons iced water	*1-2 tablespoons ice water*
Filling:	Filling:
juice of 1 lemon	*juice of 1 lemon*
350 g/12 oz crisp eating apples	*3/4 lb crisp dessert apples*
3 tablespoons milk	*3 tablespoons milk*
3 tablespoons double cream	*3 tablespoons heavy cream*
1 egg, beaten	*1 egg, beaten*
2 tablespoons soft brown sugar	*2 tablespoons light brown sugar*

1. Make the rich wholemeal (wholewheat) pastry. Sift the flour and salt into a bowl and make a well in the centre. Tip in any bran remaining in the sieve (strainer). Add the butter, egg yolk and brown sugar to the well, then work the ingredients together with the fingertips, adding the water gradually until a smooth soft dough is obtained. Leave in the refrigerator for at least 1 hour.

2. Roll out the dough on a floured surface and use to line the base and sides of a buttered 20 cm/8 inch flan tin (pie pan) with a removable base. Set aside.

3. For the filling, pour the lemon juice into a large bowl. Peel, quarter and core the apples one at a time, then slice thinly into the bowl of lemon juice, stirring to prevent discoloration.

4. Arrange the apple slices on the unbaked pastry shell in a circular pattern, working from the edge of the tin inwards and overlapping the slices slightly. Stand the flan tin on a baking sheet and bake in a preheated oven (230°C/450°F), Gas Mark 8 for 10 minutes.

5. Meanwhile, whisk all the remaining filling ingredients together in a bowl. Pour over the apples in the flan tin.

6. Reduce the oven temperature to (190°C/375°F), Gas Mark 5 and bake for a further 30 minutes. Leave to cool slightly, then serve warm. ·1·

C · O · U · N · T · D · O · W · N

On the day:
Make the salad dressing. Segment the orange and place the segments in a sealed plastic container. Make the wholemeal pastry, wrap in cling film (plastic wrap) and chill. Coat the liver slices and chill. Set the table. A young red such as Beaujolais Villages would go well with the liver.

To serve at 8 pm:
6.00: Open the red wine.
6.45: Preheat the oven to (230°C/450°F), Gas Mark 8. Roll out the pastry and line the flan tin (pie pan). Slice the apples and arrange on top of the pastry.
7.05: Bake the filled flan on a baking sheet in the oven. Make the flan topping.
7.15: Reduce oven temperature to (190°C/375°F), Gas Mark 5. Pour topping over apple flan and return the flan to the oven. Bake the jacket potatoes.
7.25: Prepare the watercress and place it in a bowl with the chopped orange segments and the hazelnuts. Pour the dressing over the salad, toss and set aside at room temperature.
7.35: Fry the onion rings for the liver dish. Keep them warm.
7.45: Remove apple flan from the oven and set aside to cool slightly. Fry the liver slices, coat with the sauce and onion rings and keep warm.
8.00: Serve salad starter.

F · R · E · E · Z · E · R · N · O · T · E · S
None of the dishes is suitable for freezing.

M · E · N · U

· 7 ·

Light Summer Lunch for 6

Curried Apple Soup

·

Wholemeal Spaghetti with Tuna Fish Sauce
Courgette and Radicchio Salad

·

Blackcurrant Kissel

What do you do when your lunch guests arrive at your home at the same time as you do? Perhaps you've spent the morning playing tennis together or watching your children compete in a school soccer match. You may have had to collect houseguests from the railway station or take Auntie Flo to the dentist. Whatever the reason, you've known in advance that this is one lunch party you couldn't spend hours over.

Plan Ahead

How do you cope? You choose our special lunch menu. The curried soup and kissel can both be made the night before.

The spaghetti and salad (a simple green salad would be just as suitable) are both made at the last minute, which means that within 45 minutes of arriving home, you can have a meal on the table that will make your reputation as a superbly organized hostess.

Should your plans change, you can easily alter the schedule to serve the meal at a later time. It can even be postponed to the evening with no ill effects.

A light red wine or a dryish rosé make perfect companions to this summer lunch. If red is your choice, select a Beaujolais – it's drinkable after a very short breather.

Curried Apple Soup

Metric/Imperial	American
50 g/2 oz butter	1/4 cup butter
750 g/1 1/2 lb cooking apples, peeled, cored and chopped	1 1/2 lb tart apples, pared, cored and chopped
2 small onions, sliced	2 small onions, sliced
3 sticks tender celery, thinly sliced	3 stalks tender celery, thinly sliced
1 tablespoon mild or hot curry powder, to taste	1 tablespoon mild or hot curry powder, to taste
1 tablespoon chopped fresh mint	1 tablespoon chopped fresh mint
3 tablespoons lemon juice	3 tablespoons lemon juice
900 ml/1 1/2 pints chicken stock	3 3/4 cups chicken stock
3 tablespoons semolina (preferably wholemeal)	3 tablespoons semolina flour (preferably wholewheat)
3 × 150 ml/5 fl oz cartons natural yogurt	1 pint unflavored yogurt
salt	salt
freshly ground black pepper	freshly ground black pepper
To Garnish:	For Garnish:
2 tablespoons sunflower seeds	2 tablespoons sunflower seeds
6 sprigs of parsley	6 sprigs of parsley

1. Melt the butter in a large pan and gently fry the apples, onions and celery, stirring occasionally, for 5 minutes. Increase the heat to moderate, stir in the curry powder and cook for 3 minutes.
2. Add the mint and lemon juice and pour on the stock, stirring. Bring slowly to the boil, cover, reduce heat and simmer for 20 minutes or until the apples are tender.
3. Purée the soup in a blender or food processor or rub through a nylon sieve (strainer).
4. Put the semolina in the rinsed pan and gradually pour on the apple purée, stirring all the time. Pour on the yogurt and bring slowly to simmering point.

Do not allow to boil. Add salt and pepper to taste.
5. Remove from the heat, cool the soup and then refrigerate until required.
6. Serve individual portions garnished with sunflower seeds and parsley sprigs and accompanied by wholemeal (wholewheat) grissini, if liked. ·2·14·

Rescue Tactic:
If the curry flavour is too overpowering simply stir in 1 or 2 extra tablespoons natural (unflavored) yogurt.

Wholemeal Spaghetti with Tuna Fish Sauce

Metric/Imperial	American
2 teaspoons salt	2 teaspoons salt
2 teaspoons vegetable oil	2 teaspoons vegetable oil
750 g/1 1/2 lb wholemeal spaghetti	1 1/2 lb wholewheat spaghetti
75 g/3 oz butter	6 tablespoons butter
1 fat clove garlic, peeled and crushed	1 fat clove garlic, peeled and crushed
3 tablespoons olive oil	3 tablespoons olive oil
300 ml/1/2 pint chicken stock	1 1/4 cups chicken stock
4 tablespoons dry sherry	1/4 cup dry sherry
3 × 99 g/3 1/2 oz cans tuna fish, drained and flaked	1 × 12 1/2 oz can chunk light tuna, drained and flaked
3 tablespoons single cream	3 tablespoons light cream
4 tablespoons parsley	4 tablespoons parsley
freshly ground black pepper	freshly ground black pepper

1. Bring a large pan of water to the boil and add the salt and vegetable oil. Cook the spaghetti for 12 to 13 minutes, or until it is just tender.
2. Drain the spaghetti in a colander and run hot water through it. Drain again, return to the pan, stir in half the butter and keep the spaghetti warm.
3. Meanwhile sauté the garlic in the olive oil and remaining butter over moderate heat for 2 minutes. Pour on the stock and sherry and boil rapidly for

5 minutes to reduce the liquid. Stir in the tuna fish and cream. Taste and adjust the seasoning if necessary.

4. Turn the spaghetti into a heated serving dish, pour on the sauce and toss lightly. Garnish with the remaining parsley. ·2·12·

Cougette and Radicchio Salad

Metric/Imperial	American
6 tablespoons Vinaigrette Dressing (see page 10)	6 tablespoons Vinaigrette Dressing (see page 10)
1 clove garlic, peeled and crushed	1 clove garlic, peeled and crushed
250 g/8 oz courgettes, thinly sliced	2 cups thinly sliced zucchini
1 head radicchio	1 head radicchio
	1/3 cup pitted ripe olives

Wholemeal spaghetti with tuna fish sauce.

50 g/2 oz black olives, stoned	1 tablespoon pignoli
1 tablespoon pine nuts	salt
salt	freshly ground black pepper
freshly ground black pepper	

1. Place the vinaigrette and garlic in a salad bowl. Add the sliced courgettes (zucchini) and toss well. Leave to stand for 30 minutes to allow the courgettes to absorb the flavour of the dressing. There is no need to refrigerate at this stage.

2. Tear the radicchio leaves into manageable pieces and add to the courgettes and dressing with the black (ripe) olives and pine nuts (pignoli).

3. Season with salt and pepper to taste. Toss the salad thoroughly before serving. ·2·8·11·

31

Blackcurrant Kissel

Metric/Imperial	American
1 kg/2 lb fresh or frozen blackcurrants	3 pints fresh or frozen black currants
125 g/4 oz soft brown sugar	2/3 cup, packed, light brown sugar
6 tablespoons red wine	6 tablespoons red wine
juice and grated rind of 1 orange	juice and grated rind of 1 orange
1½ tablespoons arrowroot	1½ tablespoons arrowroot
150 ml/5 fl oz double cream or natural yogurt, to serve	2/3 cup heavy cream or unflavored yogurt, to serve
flaked almonds, to decorate	slivered almonds, to decorate

1. In a heavy-based saucepan, cook the blackcurrants with the sugar, wine and orange juice and rind over low heat for about 8 to 10 minutes, or until the blackcurrants are just tender.

2. Stir a little of the juice from the fruit into the arrowroot to make a smooth paste. Stir this into the fruit and simmer gently, stirring all the time, until the mixture thickens.

3. Pour the kissel into a serving dish and cover with cling film (plastic wrap), pressing this onto the surface to prevent the formation of a skin.

4. When the kissel is cold, transfer it to the refrigerator.

5. Just before serving, whip the cream if using. Decorate the kissel with flaked (slivered) almonds and serve with cream or yogurt.

Cook's Tip:

Any leftover kissel makes a delicious sauce with ice cream, particularly if you top it with lightly toasted almonds.

C · O · U · N · T · D · O · W · N

The day before:

Prepare the Curried Apple Soup up to the end of stage 6. Cover with cling film (plastic wrap) and chill. Make the salad dressing. Store in a cool place but do not refrigerate. Make the Blackcurrant Kissel. Cover and refrigerate until required.

On the day:

Set the table, do the flowers and chill the white wines. A Verdicchio would be a happy choice to accompany the pasta. Serve a Sauternes with the dessert.

To serve at 1 pm:

12.15 Wash the radicchio. Dry the leaves in a salad spinner or between sheets of absorbent kitchen paper. Wash and slice the courgettes (zucchini). Halve the olives. Place the ingredients in a large salad bowl.

12.30: Prepare the salad up to the end of stage 1. Chill six soup bowls.

12.35: Bring a large pan of water to the boil.

12.40: Add salt and oil to the pan and cook the spaghetti until it is just done – or *al dente*. While it is cooking, prepare the sauce.

12.52/3: Drain the spaghetti, rinse under hot water and drain again. Add butter and keep hot.

12.55: Spoon the soup into six chilled bowls and garnish with sunflower seeds and parsley sprigs. Take the white wine to the table in a bucket of iced water.

1.00: Preheat the grill (broiler). Serve the chilled soup with wholemeal (wholewheat) grissini, if liked.

Between courses: Toss the spaghetti with the sauce and garnish with the remaining parsley to serve.

Complete the salad, toss well so that all the leaves are well coated with the dressing and serve. Drizzle 1 tablespoon of the cream or yoghurt over the surface of the kissel. Whip the cream. Decorate the kissel and serve with the cream or natural (unflavored) yogurt and the Sauternes.

F · R · E · E · Z · E · R · N · O · T · E · S

Pack and freeze the Blackcurrant Kissel at the end of stage 4. Thaw overnight in the refrigerator and finish as per recipe.

MENU

· 8 ·

Sunday Lunch for 6

Endive Salad

·

Deep Dish Vegetable Pie
Jacket Potatoes with Cheese and Herb Filling

·

Apricot Mould

When it comes to Sunday lunch, fruit and vegetables are all too often cast in a supporting role. In this colourful menu they star in a range of dishes designed to show off their versatility.

To launch the lunch, there's a simply delicious Endive (Chicory) Salad with peppers and peanuts. To follow, a Deep Dish Vegetable Pie with a chorus line that includes carrots, corn, courgettes (zucchini) and cauliflower. This is served with baked jacket potatoes with a creamy Brie filling. Tender wedges of steamed cabbage can also be served for those with extra large appetites.

The final act introduces a light and delicately flavoured Apricot Mould served with golden brown meringues, topped as a finale with whipped cream.

Vegetarians in View

The menu wasn't formulated for vegetarians, but you may happily serve it to them. Substitute agar-agar for the gelatine in the dessert and, if your guests object to eating cheese soured with rennet, omit the Brie from their jacket potatoes.

You may be certain that, at the end of the meal, the curtain will come down to thunderous applause.

Endive Salad

Metric/Imperial	American
2 green peppers, cored, seeded and thinly sliced	2 green peppers, seeded and thinly sliced
1 yellow pepper, cored, seeded and thinly sliced	1 yellow pepper, seeded and thinly sliced
1 red pepper, cored, seeded and thinly sliced	1 red pepper, seeded and thinly sliced
2 small onions, cut into rings	2 small onions, cut into rings
1 medium endive, torn into pieces	1 medium head chicory, torn into pieces
2 tablespoons chopped fresh mint	2 tablespoons chopped fresh mint
3 tablespoons unsalted peanuts	3 tablespoons unsalted peanuts
Dressing:	Dressing:
1 hard-boiled egg yolk	1 hard-cooked egg yolk
4 tablespoons olive oil	1/4 cup olive oil
1 tablespoon cider vinegar	1 tablespoon cider vinegar
1 clove garlic, peeled and crushed	1 clove garlic, peeled and crushed
salt	salt
freshly ground black pepper	freshly ground black pepper

1. First make the dressing. Mash the egg yolk in a bowl, then gradually add the oil, stirring constantly. Stir in the vinegar, garlic and salt and pepper to taste and mix well.
2. Mix the pepper strips together in a large shallow bowl, add the dressing and toss to coat. Cover and set aside to marinate for 1 hour. There is no need to refrigerate at this stage.
3. Place the onions, endive (chicory) and mint in a salad bowl. Chill. Just before serving, pour over the peppers and dressing and toss well. Scatter the peanuts on top.

Deep-dish vegetable pie; Jacket potatoes; Steamed cabbage wedges.

Deep Dish Vegetable Pie

Metric/Imperial	American
25 g/1 oz butter	2 tablespoons butter
1 teaspoon each cumin and coriander seeds, crushed	1 teaspoon each cumin and coriander seeds, crushed
500 g/1 lb small carrots, quartered lengthways	1 lb baby carrots, quartered lengthwise
1 × 312 g/11 oz can sweetcorn kernels, drained	1 × 12 oz can whole kernel corn, drained
1 medium cauliflower, cut into florets	1 medium cauliflower, cut into flowerets
250 g/8 oz turnips, diced	1½ cups diced turnips
250 g/8 oz courgettes,	2 cups thickly sliced zucchini

thickly sliced
250 g/8 oz shelled broad
  beans
250 g/8 oz young French
  beans
300 ml/½ pint water
salt
Sauce:
40 g/1½ oz butter
1 medium onion, chopped
2 cloves garlic, peeled and
  crushed
1 tablespoon curry powder
1½ tablespoons wholemeal
  flour
300 ml/½ pint single
  cream
salt
freshly ground black pepper
2 tablespoons chopped
  parsley
250 g/8 oz Rich
  Wholemeal Pastry (see
  page 28, omit sugar)

1½ cups hulled fava beans
½ lb young green beans
1¼ cups water
salt
Sauce:
3 tablespoons butter
1 medium onion, chopped
2 cloves garlic, peeled and
  crushed
1 tablespoon curry powder
1½ tablespoons wholewheat
  flour
1¼ cups light cream
salt
freshly ground black pepper
2 tablespoons chopped
  parsley
250 g/8 oz Rich
  Wholewheat Pastry (see
  page 28, omit sugar)

1. Heat the butter in a large pan and fry the cumin and coriander seeds with all the vegetables except the corn and cook until lightly browned. Stir in the water and salt. Bring to the boil, cover, and simmer until the vegetables are just tender. Drain, reserving the cooking liquid.
2. To make the sauce, melt the butter in a large saucepan and sauté the onion and garlic for 3 minutes, stirring occasionally. Stir in the curry powder and flour and cook for 1 minute. Add 120 ml/4 fl oz (½ cup) of the vegetable cooking water and stir. Add the cream and stir until the sauce thickens. Season to taste. Stir the vegetables and parsley into the sauce, together with the corn, and mix well.
3. Place a pie funnel in the centre of a 2 litre/3½

pint (9 cup) deep pie dish. Spoon the vegetables and sauce into the dish and leave to cool.
4. Roll out the pastry on a lightly floured board. Cut a strip of dough to fit the rim of the dish. Dampen the rim and press on the pastry strip. Cover the dish with the remaining dough and press to the strip on the rim. Trim the edges and flute them. Brush the pastry with beaten egg. Re-roll the trimmings and cut out leaf shapes. Arrange them on the pie and brush with beaten egg.
5. Stand the dish on a baking sheet. Bake in a preheated oven (200°C/400°F), Gas Mark 6 for 20 to 25 minutes or until the top is golden brown. Serve hot, with the filled jacket potatoes and steamed cabbage wedges. ·4·

Jacket Potatoes with Cheese and Herb Filling

Metric/Imperial	American
6 large potatoes, scrubbed	6 large potatoes, scrubbed
oil for brushing	oil for brushing
150 ml/¼ pint soured cream	⅔ cup sour cream
75 g/3 oz Brie cheese	3 oz Brie cheese
freshly ground black pepper	freshly ground black pepper
2 tablespoons spring onions	2 tablespoons scallions
1 tablespoon chopped parsley	1 tablespoon chopped parsley

1. Prick the potatoes all over and brush the skins with oil. Bake them in their jackets in a preheated oven (200°C/400°F), Gas Mark 6 for about 1 hour. Test with a skewer.
2. Place the soured cream and Brie in a blender or food processor and purée. Stir in the herbs.
3. When the potatoes are cooked, cut a thin slice from one long side and scoop out the 'flesh'. Beat in the cheese and herb mixture. Spoon the mixture back into the potato shells.
4. Replace the potato 'lids' and return them to the oven (200°C/400°F), Gas Mark 6 for 5 minutes.

Apricot Mould

Metric/Imperial	American
250 g/8 oz dried apricots, soaked overnight	1/2 lb dried apricots, soaked overnight
thinly pared strip of orange rind	thinly pared strip of orange rind
75 g/3 oz soft brown sugar	1/2 cup light brown sugar
150 ml/1/4 pint unsweetened orange juice	2/3 cup unsweetened orange juice
15 g/1/2 oz powdered gelatine	1 1/2 envelopes unflavored gelatin
2 egg whites, stiffly beaten	2 egg whites, stiffly beaten
Meringue:	Meringue:
2 egg whites	2 egg whites
125 g/4 oz soft brown sugar	2/3 cup light brown sugar
whipped cream, to serve	whipped cream, to serve

1. Put the apricots and 600 ml/1 pint (2 1/2 cups) soaking liquid into a saucepan with the orange rind. Bring to the boil, reduce the heat, cover the pan and simmer for four minutes, or until the apricots are tender. Discard the orange rind.
2. Purée the apricots and liquid in a blender or food processor or rub them through a sieve (strainer). Return the purée to the pan. Add the sugar and stir over a low heat until it has dissolved. Simmer for 10 minutes.
3. Put the orange juice into a small heatproof bowl, sprinkle over the gelatine and stand the bowl in a pan of hot water. Stir to dissolve the gelatine. Stir the gelatine mixture into the apricot purée. Let the mixture cool slightly, then fold in the stiffly beaten egg whites.
4. Rinse a 900 ml/1 1/2 pint (2 quart) mould with cold water. Pour in the apricot mixture and set aside to cool. Chill for at least 2 hours or until set.
5. Make the meringues. Beat the egg whites until stiff. Gradually beat in the sugar and continue beating until the mixture is stiff again.

6. Line a baking sheet with two layers of lightly greased greaseproof (waxed) paper or with non-stick silicone paper. Use a teaspoon to put blobs of the meringue mixture onto the paper.
7. Bake the meringues in a preheated oven (120°C/250°F), Gas Mark 1/2 for 1 1/2 hours or until they are crisp and dry. Peel the meringues from the paper and cool. Store in an airtight container.
8. When ready to serve, turn out the apricot mould and top it with the meringue. Serve with whipped cream.

Variations:
If cooking for vegetarians, substitute 3 teaspoons agar-agar for the gelatine.

C · O · U · N · T · D · O · W · N

The day before:
Place the apricots for the mould in a large bowl, pour over water to cover and soak overnight. Make the meringues. Store in an airtight container.

On the day:
Make the Apricot Mould. Make the salad dressing. Make the wholemeal (wholewheat) pastry. Prepare the Deep Dish Vegetable Pie up to the end of stage 3. Make the cheese and sour cream filling. Set out the wines. We suggest a Muscadet or Alsace Sylvaner.

To serve at 1 pm:
11.25: Preheat the oven.
11.30: Prepare the vegetables for the salad.
11.55: Bake the jacket potatoes.
12.00: Chill the white wine. Pour the salad dressing over the pepper slices. Toss well. Cover with cling film and marinate for 1 hour. Whip the cream to serve with the Apricot Mould. Cover and refrigerate. Make the pie crust.
12.35: Place the pie in the oven.
12.45: Turn out the Apricot Mould onto a serving plate and return it to the refrigerator.
12.50: Combine all salad ingredients and toss. Finish the potatoes.
1.00: Serve the meal. Take the wines to the table.

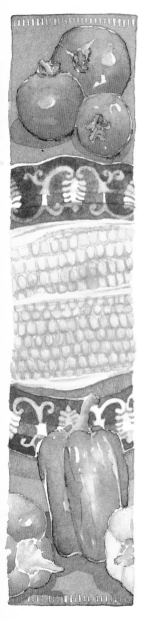

· 9 ·

Casual Supper for 4

Red Bean Pâté with Wholemeal Toast

·

Lentil and Watercress Patties
Brown Rice with Crisp Vegetables

·

Baked Stuffed Peaches

Quick 'n' Easy

Here's a menu that requires the minimum of attention, so its ideal for any occasion when you want to avoid spending long hours in the kitchen – Wimbledon fortnight, perhaps or the night you celebrate successfully completing a marathon!

The pâté and lentil patties are cooked ahead, the latter needing only a few minutes of your time just before serving. Any left-over patties can be enjoyed cold with salad for a light lunch or picnic snack. The brown rice will demand some attention during the hour preceding the meal, but shouldn't tax you unduly. Make sure all the ingredients are prepared and ready to cook. The dessert – baked peaches, stuffed with ground almonds – is as easy to prepare as it is to enjoy.

Once again, the emphasis is on high-fibre cooking. The pâté is a particularly good source of fibre, especially when accompanied by wholemeal (wholewheat) toast; so is the lentil dish. Incidentally, lentils are also a good source of iron.

Should your plans change, you can easily alter the time plan to serve the meal earlier for a light lunch. A dry Italian red or a Rioja would go particularly well with these dishes. Remember to open the bottles about two hours before serving.

Red Bean Pâté

Metric/Imperial	American
2 rashers bacon, chopped	2 bacon slices, chopped
1 small onion, diced	1 small onion, diced
1 clove garlic, peeled and crushed	1 clove garlic, peeled and crushed
1 × 425 g/15 oz can red kidney beans, drained	1 × 16 oz can red kidney beans, drained
1 tablespoon tomato purée	1 tablespoon tomato paste
2 tablespoons water	2 tablespoons water
1 teaspoon lemon juice	1 teaspoon lemon juice
salt	salt
freshly ground black pepper	freshly ground black pepper
wholemeal toast, to serve	wholewheat toast, to serve

1. Fry the bacon in a small saucepan over low heat until the fat runs. Then increase the heat to moderate and add the onion and garlic. Cook for 2 to 3 minutes until the onion is soft and the bacon crisp.
2. Add the remaining ingredients and cook over moderate heat for 5 minutes, stirring all the time.
3. Purée in a blender or food processor until smooth. Spoon into four individual ramekins, cover with cling film (plastic wrap) and chill until required. Serve with hot wholemeal (wholewheat) toast. ·1·10·

Lentil and Watercress Patties

Metric/Imperial	American
1 large onion, finely chopped	1 large onion, finely chopped
2 cloves garlic, peeled and crushed	2 cloves garlic, peeled and crushed
3 tablespoons vegetable oil	3 tablespoons vegetable oil
250 g/8 oz split red lentils, washed and drained	1 cup split red lentils, washed and drained
600 ml/1 pint chicken or vegetable stock	2½ cups chicken or vegetable stock
few sprigs of parsley	few sprigs of parsley
2 tablespoons tomato purée	2 tablespoons tomato paste
125 g/4 oz blanched almonds, chopped	1 cup chopped almonds
1 bunch of watercress sprigs, finely chopped	1 bunch of watercress sprigs, finely chopped
1 tablespoon chopped mint	1 tablespoon chopped mint
salt	salt
freshly ground black pepper	freshly ground black pepper
2 tablespoons wholemeal flour	2 tablespoons wholewheat flour
oil for frying	oil for frying
To Garnish:	For Garnish:
shredded lettuce	shredded lettuce
tomato wedges	tomato wedges
spring onions	scallions

1. Sauté the onion and garlic in the oil over moderate heat for 2 minutes. Add the lentils and stir to coat them with oil.
2. Pour on the stock, add the parsley and bring to the boil. Lower the heat, cover and simmer for 40 minutes. The lentils should be soft and have absorbed the stock. If there is some liquid, increase the heat to evaporate it. Discard the parsley and remove the pan from the heat.
3. Beat the tomato purée (paste) into the lentils, almonds, watercress and mint. Season.
4. When cool enough to handle, divide the mixture into 12 and mould into flat 'burger' shapes. Toss them in the flour. Cover and chill in the refrigerator for at least 1 hour before frying.
5. Fry the patties in hot oil over moderate heat for about 5 minutes on each side, or until they are crisp. Serve hot. ·4·5·

Cook's Tip:
Try the Lentil and Watercress Patties cold, as a light lunch with salad.

Brown rice with crisp vegetables; Lentil and watercress patties.

Brown Rice with Crisp Vegetables

Metric/Imperial	American
1 medium onion, sliced	1 medium onion, sliced
2 cloves garlic, peeled and crushed	2 cloves garlic, peeled and crushed
2 tablespoons olive oil	2 tablespoons olive oil
350 g/12 oz brown long-grain rice	1½ cups brown long-grain rice

900 ml/1½ pints hot chicken stock	3¾ cups hot chicken stock
salt	salt
freshly ground black pepper	freshly ground black pepper
1 small cauliflower, cut into small florets	1 small cauliflower, cut into small flowerets
250 g/8 oz carrots, scraped and finely diced	1½ cups finely diced scraped carrots
2 leeks, sliced	2 leeks, sliced
125 g/4 oz shelled peas	¾ cup hulled peas
25 g/1 oz butter	2 tablespoons butter
125 g/4 oz Cheddar cheese, grated	1 cup grated Cheddar cheese
1 tablespoon chopped fresh mint	1 tablespoon chopped fresh mint
1 tablespoon chopped fresh parsley	1 tablespoon chopped fresh parsley
grated Parmesan cheese, to serve	grated Parmesan cheese, to serve
sprigs of fresh mint, to garnish	sprigs of fresh mint, for garnish

1. In a heavy-based saucepan, sauté the onion and garlic in the oil for 2 minutes. Stir in the rice and cook for 1 minute ensuring that each grain of rice is well coated with the oil.

2. Pour on the hot stock, season and bring to the boil. Cover, lower the heat and simmer for 40 minutes. The rice should be just tender and have absorbed all the stock.

3. While the rice is cooking, steam the cauliflower, carrots, leeks and peas for about 10 to 12 minutes, or until just tender.

4. Melt the butter in another pan and sauté the vegetables, stirring frequently, for about 4 minutes, until they are glazed but not brown.

5. Stir the vegetables, Cheddar cheese and mint into the cooked rice. Sprinkle with the parsley. Hand the Parmesan cheese separately. Garnish the brown rice and crisp vegetables with sprigs of mint and serve piping hot.

Baked Stuffed Peaches

Metric/Imperial	American
4 large firm, ripe peaches	4 large firm, ripe peaches
50 g/2 oz cake crumbs, preferably wholemeal	1 cup cake crumbs, preferably wholewheat
50 g/2 oz ground almonds	½ cup finely ground almonds
50 g/2 oz soft brown sugar	⅓ cup, packed, light brown sugar
25 g/1 oz butter, softened	2 tablespoons softened butter
juice of 1 lemon	juice of 1 lemon
natural yogurt (optional), to serve	unflavored yogurt (optional), to serve

1. Dip the peaches in boiling water for a few seconds to loosen their skins. Drain and plunge into cold water. Peel, halve and remove the stones (seeds). Using a teaspoon, scoop enough flesh from each half to make a deep indentation for the stuffing. Chop the peach flesh.
2. Mix the peach flesh with the cake crumbs, nuts, sugar, butter and lemon juice to moisten. Pile the stuffing into the peach halves and smooth the tops. Arrange the peaches, side by side in a shallow buttered ovenproof dish. If not baking immediately, brush any exposed cut surfaces with lemon juice and cover tightly with cling film (plastic wrap).
3. Bake the peaches in a preheated oven (180°C/350°F), Gas Mark 4 for 30 to 35 minutes. Serve warm, with natural (unflavored) yogurt if desired.
·13·

C · O · U · N · T · D · O · W · N

The day before:
Make the red bean pâté. Cover with cling film (plastic wrap) and refrigerate.
On the day:
Prepare the Lentil and Watercress Patties up to the end of stage 4. Grate the Cheddar cheese for the rice dish and store in a plastic bag in the refrigerator.

Chop the mint and parsley and store in the same way. Lay the table (or organize trays if you're going to enjoy a lazy lap-supper). Do the flowers.
About 6 pm: Open the wine. A dry Italian red or a Rioja would go well with this meal.
6.30: Stuff the peaches and place, tightly covered, in the refrigerator until required.
7.00: Prepare the vegetables for the brown rice dish. Preheat the oven to (180°C/350°F), Gas Mark 4.
7.10: Steam the cauliflower, carrot, leeks and peas. As soon as they are tender (but still crisp), remove them from the heat and immediately plunge them into iced water to arrest further cooking. Drain on absorbent kitchen paper and set aside.
7.20: Pop the peaches into the oven to bake.
7.30: Start cooking the brown rice.
7.40: Fry the lentil patties, draining them on absorbent kitchen paper and keeping them hot until ready to serve.
7.55: Make the wholemeal (wholewheat) toast. Remove the baked peaches from the oven and keep warm in a foil tent.
8.00: Serve the pâté and toast.
Between courses: Finish the rice dish by melting the butter and glazing the steamed vegetables. Combine with the remaining ingredients and serve with the lentil patties. Spoon yogurt into a small bowl to serve with the dessert, if liked.

F · R · E · E · Z · E · R · N · O · T · E · S

Pack and freeze the Red Bean Pâté. Thaw overnight in the refrigerator. Wrap and freeze the Lentil and Watercress Patties at the end of stage 4. Thaw overnight in the refrigerator and finish as per recipe.
Cook's Tip:
Cook, cool and freeze the rice for Brown Rice with Crisp Vegetables. Thaw overnight in the refrigerator. Sauté the vegetables in a large pan and stir in the defrosted rice at the end of stage 4. Cook, stirring for 1 to 2 minutes until hot through. Finish with the cheese and herbs as directed.

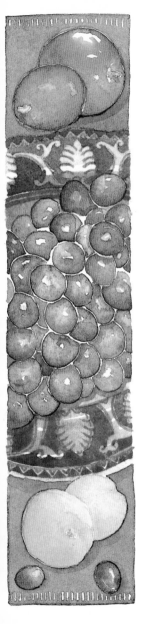

MENU

· 10 ·

Beginners Please – Simple Dinner for 4

Grilled Corn on the Cob

·

Pork Chops with Lentils
Wholemeal Potato Cakes
Red Bean and Calabrese Salad

·

Tangy Apple Pudding

When you're a comparative newcomer to the kitchen, giving a dinner party can be rather daunting. Do you serve something cheap and cheerful, like spaghetti bolognese, or do you go all out to impress and stretch both imagination and bank balance to the hilt?

Advance Preparation

We suggest you take the middle path. Choose a menu you know you can handle with ease. Do as much as you can in advance, and use the timetable for the last-minute preparation. Tack it up somewhere near the cooker. Not only will it ensure that nothing is forgotten, it will also be an enormous confidence-booster.

Keep It Simple

The main course is a pork casserole, with lentils adding extra interest (and that all-important fibre). It will simmer quite happily while you greet your guests. The accompaniments are a marinated salad, made in advance, and Wholemeal Potato Cakes.

The pudding is a triumph of contrasting colours and textures – puréed apples and apricots with oats, cream and chocolate.

Grilled Corn on the Cob

Metric/Imperial	American
4 fresh corn on the cob	4 fresh corn on the cob
pinch of cayenne pepper	pinch of cayenne
salt	salt
freshly ground black pepper	freshly ground black pepper
125 g/4 oz butter	1/2 cup butter

1. Remove the husks and silky threads from the corn. Bring a large pan of water to the boil, add the corn and cayenne, lower the heat and cook for about 8 to 10 minutes, or until tender. Drain the cobs thoroughly and season to taste with salt and pepper.
2. Meanwhile, melt the butter in a small saucepan. Place the corn on a grill (broiler) rack over a drip tray. Cook under a preheated hot grill (broiler) until golden brown on every side, turning and brushing regularly with melted butter.
3. To serve, arrange the corn on the cobs on a warm serving dish and pour over the butter from the drip tray. Serve immediately. ·1·4·

Cook's Tip:
Do not add salt to the water used for cooking corn on the cob – it toughens the kernels.

Pork Chops with Lentils

Metric/Imperial	American
500 g/1 lb green lentils	2 cups green lentils
1 bay leaf	1 bay leaf
2 onions, peeled but left whole	2 onions, peeled but left whole
1 whole clove	1 whole clove
salt	salt
freshly ground black pepper	freshly ground black pepper
4 pork chops, trimmed of fat	4 pork chops, trimmed of fat
4 fresh sage leaves, chopped	4 fresh sage leaves, chopped
50 g/2 oz butter	1/4 cup butter
4 small sausages	4 small sausage links
2 carrots, diced	2 carrots, diced
about 600 ml/1 pint chicken stock	about 2 1/2 cups chicken stock

1. Wash the lentils under cold running water and pick them over to remove any grit. Place in a large pan with the bay leaf and 1 onion stuck with the clove. Cover with water, bring to the boil, reduce the heat and simmer for 1 hour. After 30 minutes add salt and pepper to taste.
2. Meanwhile sprinkle the chops with the sage and salt and pepper to taste. Melt the butter in a large flameproof casserole, add the chops and cook over brisk heat for 10 minutes until browned on all sides. Remove with a slotted spoon and set aside.
3. Prick the sausage skins with a fork. Chop the remaining onion. Add to the casserole with the carrots and cook over brisk heat for 10 minutes until lightly coloured, stirring constantly.
4. Drain the lentils, then add to the casserole with the chops. Cover with the stock and bring to the boil. Lower the heat, cover and cook gently for 1 hour or until the chops are tender.
5. Taste and adjust the seasoning. Remove the chops and sausages from the casserole and arrange around the edge of a warm serving platter. Pile the lentils in the centre. Serve immediately. ·9·

Wholemeal Potato Cakes

Metric/Imperial	American
500 g/1 lb potatoes, boiled and mashed	1 lb potatoes, boiled and mashed
50 g/2 oz butter	1/4 cup butter
salt	salt
freshly ground black pepper	freshly ground black pepper
125 g/4 oz wholemeal flour	1 cup wholewheat flour

1. In a large bowl, beat together the potatoes, butter, salt and pepper. Add enough flour to make a malleable dough.

2. Divide the dough in half and pat or roll each piece to a round about 1 cm/½ inch thick.

3. Cut each round into 8 triangles. If not required immediately, place these on a floured plate, cover with cling film (plastic wrap) and keep in the refrigerator for up to 8 hours before frying.

4. Heat a heavy-based frying pan (skillet) and grease thoroughly. Transfer the potato cakes carefully to the frying pan and cook for 5 minutes on each side. Keep warm in a folded tea towel. ·6·

Red Bean and Calabrese Salad

Metric/Imperial	American
250 g/8 oz dried red kidney beans	1 scant cup dried red kidney beans
900 ml/1½ pints water	3¾ cups water
250 g/8 oz calabrese or broccoli, broken into florets	½ lb calabrese or broccoli, broken into flowerets
150 ml/¼ pint Vinaigrette Dressing (see page 10)	⅔ cup Vinaigrette Dressing (see page 10)
2 celery sticks, thinly sliced	2 celery stalks, thinly sliced
2 spring onions, thinly sliced	2 scallions, thinly sliced

1. Soak the beans in the water overnight. Drain.

2. Transfer the beans with fresh water to a large saucepan, bring to the boil and boil rapidly for 10 minutes. Cover, reduce the heat and simmer for 1 to 1½ hours until tender. Drain.

3. Divide the calabrese into florets. Blanch in boiling water for 1 minute. Drain and cool.

4. Place the warm, cooked beans in a mixing bowl

Red bean and calabrese salad

and pour the vinaigrette over. Add the calabrese, celery and onions (scallions) and toss thoroughly.

5. Leave to marinate at room temperature for a few hours. Stir before serving. ·6·

Cook's Tip:
To save time, substitute 1 × 425 g (15 oz) can red kidney beans, drained, for the boiled beans.

Tangy Apple Pudding

Metric/Imperial	American
750 g/1½ lb cooking apples	1½ lb tart apples
250 g/8 oz dried apricots, soaked overnight in water	1½ cups dried apricots, soaked overnight in water
brown sugar to taste	brown sugar to taste
Topping:	Topping:
75 g/3 oz butter	6 tablespoons butter
125 g/4 oz rolled oats	1⅓ cups rolled oats
50 g/2 oz demerara sugar	⅓ cup, packed, brown sugar
150 ml/¼ pint double cream	⅔ cup heavy cream
4 tablespoons grated chocolate, to decorate	4 tablespoons grated chocolate, to decorate

1. Peel and slice the apples and place in a saucepan with the apricots and 2-3 tablespoons of soaking liquid. Cook gently until the apricots are soft and the apples form a stiff purée. Remove from the heat, add brown sugar to taste and allow the mixture to cool.

2. Make the topping. Melt the butter in a frying pan (skillet). Add the rolled oats and cook over a gentle heat for several minutes, stirring constantly. Add the demerara sugar, blend thoroughly, then remove from the heat and cool.

3. Assemble the pudding. Spoon the fruit mixture into a serving dish and sprinkle the oat mixture on top. Whip the cream and spoon over the oat mixture. Sprinkle with the grated chocolate and serve well chilled.

C · O · U · N · T · D · O · W · N

The day before:
Place the beans for the salad in a large bowl. Add 900 ml/1½ pints (3¾ cups) cold water and soak overnight. Place the dried apricots in a second bowl, add water to cover and soak overnight.

On the day:
Cook the red beans. While they are cooking, break the calabrese into florets and slice the celery and spring onions (scallions). As soon as the beans are cooked, drain and add the remaining salad ingredients. Leave to marinate in a cool place. Prepare the Pork Chops with Lentils to the end of stage 1. Set the lentils aside, covered. Make the Wholemeal (Wholewheat) Potato Cakes to the end of stage 3. Make the Tangy Apple Pudding. Chill until required. Lay the table, do the flowers, select the wines. The homely pork dish deserves a young red burgundy, such as Beaune or Savigny. If you would prefer to serve a white wine try a dry Alsace Sylvaner.

To serve at 8 pm:
About 6: Open the red wine.

6.40: Carry on preparing the Pork Chops with Lentils. Fry the chops, sausages and vegetables and add the reserved lentils.

7.00: Turn down the heat under the pork casserole and simmer, stirring occasionally, until ready to serve. Chill the white wine, if serving. Prepare and clean the fresh corn.

7.35: Bring a large pan of water to the boil.

7.40: Cook the corn on the cob with the cayenne. Preheat the grill (broiler) to high.

7.50: Grill (broil) the corn on the cob. Fry the potato cakes, drain on absorbent kitchen paper and keep warm in a folded tea towel.

8.00: Sprinkle the corn with salt, drizzle with butter and serve. Take the wines to the table. Toss the salad in readiness for the main course.

F · R · E · E · Z · E · R · N · O · T · E · S

None of the recipes is suitable for freezing.

H · I · G · H · F · I · B · R · E

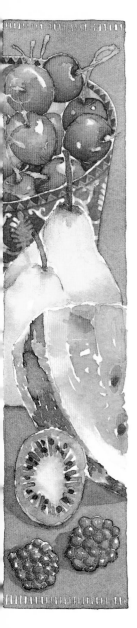

∿°M·E·N·U∿°

· 11 ·

Budget Supper for 6

Chilli con Carne
Wholemeal Soda Bread
Cucumber Sesame Salad

·

Plums in Port Wine
Sugared Walnut Biscuits

Entertaining doesn't have to be an extravagant affair. Making a meal for friends is a labour of love and what matters most is the mix of people, not the amount of money you spend on the ingredients.

Of course, when you are feeling flush or celebrating a special occasion, it is great to splash out a little, but don't deny yourself good company on the grounds that you can't afford it.

Cost Cutters

We've selected a budget menu that won't break the bank. The meal centres around that perennial favourite, Chilli con Carne. It requires only 650 g (1¼ lb) of beef to serve six, thanks to the wonderfully elastic properties of kidney beans, and is served with another cost cutter, Wholemeal Soda Bread.

Chilli con Carne is often topped with a dollop of soured cream, but in our menu the cream comes with a cucumber and sesame salad, which is the perfect accompaniment.

For the finale, present plums in port. If you make this dessert when plums are plentiful, it should not be too expensive. We suggest serving the plums with wholemeal walnut biscuits (cookies). If you think this might stretch your finances a bit too far, you could omit the biscuits.

Chilli con Carne

Metric/Imperial

250 g/8 oz dried red
  kidney beans or haricot
  beans or 1 × 425 g/
  15 oz can red kidney
  beans
3 tablespoons corn oil
2-3 medium onions,
  chopped
2 cloves garlic, peeled and
  crushed
1 green pepper, cored, seeded
  and diced
650 g/1¼ lb minced beef
2 teaspoons-2 tablespoons
  mild chilli powder
pinch of ground cumin

American

¾ cup dried red kidney
  beans or 1 cup navy
  beans or 1 × 16 oz can
  red kidney beans
3 tablespoons corn oil
2-3 medium onions,
  chopped
2 cloves garlic, peeled and
  crushed
1 green pepper, seeded and
  chopped
2½ cups ground beef
2 teaspoons-2 tablespoons
  mild chili powder
pinch of ground cumin
2 tablespoons tomato paste

2 tablespoons tomato purée
450 ml/¾ pint beef stock
4 large tomatoes, skinned
  and chopped
salt
freshly ground black pepper

2 cups beef stock
4 large tomatoes, peeled and
  chopped
salt
freshly ground black pepper

1. If using dried beans, soak them overnight, then cook them, following the instructions in stages 1 and 2 of the Red Bean and Calabrese Salad on page 43.
2. Heat the oil in a large saucepan and sauté the onions until soft. Add the beef and continue cooking, stirring, until well browned.
3. Stir in the chilli powder and cumin, together with the tomato purée (paste), stock and tomatoes. Add the well-drained beans and bring the mixture to the boil. Reduce the heat, cover and simmer for about 1½ hours, stirring occasionally and adding a little water or beef stock if the mixture is too thick.

Chilli con carne

Wholemeal Soda Bread

Metric/Imperial	American
250 g/8 oz wholemeal flour	2 cups wholewheat flour
250 g/8 oz plain flour	2 cups all-purpose flour
1 teaspoon salt	1 teaspoon salt
2 teaspoons bicarbonate of soda	2 teaspoons baking soda
2 teaspoons cream of tartar	2 teaspoons cream of tartar
50 g/2 oz white vegetable fat, cut into pieces	¼ cup vegetable shortening, cut into pieces
300 ml/½ pint buttermilk or soured milk	1¼ cups buttermilk or sour milk

1. Sift the flours together into a warmed mixing bowl with the salt, soda and cream of tartar.
2. Rub (cut) in the lard (shortening) until the mixture resembles breadcrumbs. Bind the mixture together with the buttermilk or soured milk.
3. Shape the dough into a round and place it on a greased baking sheet. Slash the surface with a sharp knife, sprinkle it with flour and bake in a preheated oven (220°C/425°F), Gas Mark 7 for about 25 minutes.
4. Turn out and cool on a wire rack. ·1·

Cucumber Sesame Salad

Metric/Imperial	American
3 cucumbers, peeled and thinly sliced	3 cucumbers, pared and thinly sliced
120 ml/4 fl oz cider vinegar	½ cup cider vinegar
2 tablespoons salt	2 tablespoons salt
50 g/2 oz creamed coconut milk	2 oz creamed coconut milk
150 ml/¼ pint double cream	⅔ cup heavy cream
½ teaspoon sugar	½ teaspoon sugar
	1 tablespoon sesame oil
	2 tablespoons chopped chives
1 tablespoon sesame oil	1 tablespoon toasted sesame seeds
2 tablespoons chopped chives	1 tablespoon chopped parsley
1 tablespoon toasted sesame seeds	
1 tablespoon chopped parsley	

1. Cover the cucumber with vinegar and salt and leave to marinate for 1 hour.
2. Drain the cucumber and transfer it to a serving bowl. In a measuring jug, mix the creamed coconut with enough milk to make 120 ml/4 fl oz (½ cup) coconut cream.
3. Whip the double (heavy) cream until it forms soft peaks. Fold in the coconut cream, sugar, and the sesame oil.
4. Pour over the cucumber and sprinkle with chives, sesame seeds and chopped parsley. Serve. ·12·

Plums in Port Wine

Metric/Imperial	American
1 kg/2 lb Victoria plums	2 lb prune plums
75 g/3 oz soft brown sugar or more to taste	½ cup, packed, light brown sugar or more to taste
120 ml/4 fl oz port wine	½ cup port wine
150 ml/¼ pint double cream, lightly whipped, to serve	⅔ cup heavy cream, lightly whipped, to serve

1. Make a slit in each plum, following the natural division of the fruit. Remove the stones (seeds) and place the fruit in a deep ovenproof baking dish. Sprinkle over the sugar.
2. Pour over the port and bake, uncovered, in a preheated oven (150°C/300°F), Gas Mark 2 for 45 minutes. Cool slightly and taste. Add more sugar if required, stirring it lightly but thoroughly into the syrup. Try not to break up the fruit.
3. Let the dish cool completely, then cover it with a lid or cling film (plastic wrap) and chill in the refrigerator until required. ·8·

Sugared Walnut Biscuits

Metric/Imperial	American
75 g/3 oz wholemeal flour	¾ cup wholewheat flour
50 g/2 oz butter	¼ cup butter
40 g/1½ oz walnuts, ground	⅓ cup ground walnuts
50 g/2 oz soft brown sugar	⅓ cup, packed, light brown sugar
1 teaspoon grated orange rind	1 teaspoon grated orange rind
1 egg, separated	1 egg, separated
2 teaspoons sherry	2 teaspoons sherry
approximately 2 teaspoons orange juice	approximately 2 teaspoons orange juice
brown sugar crystals, for topping	brown sugar crystals, for topping

1. Sift the flour into a mixing bowl. Tip in any bran remaining in the sieve (strainer). Rub (cut) in the butter until the mixture resembles breadcrumbs. Mix in the nuts, sugar and orange rind.
2. Beat the egg yolk and sherry together and add to the flour mixture together with enough orange juice to make a fairly stiff dough.
3. Roll out the dough to a rough rectangle about 1 cm/½ inch thick, cut into rounds with a fluted 5 cm/2 inch cutter and place on a greased baking sheet.
4. Beat the egg white until liquid, then brush it over the biscuits (cookies). Sprinkle with brown sugar crystals. Bake in a preheated oven (180°C/350°F), Gas Mark 4 for 15 to 20 minutes until golden. Cool on a wire rack and store in an airtight container. ·4·

C · O · U · N · T · D · O · W · N

The day before:
If using dried beans for the Chilli con Carne, soak them overnight in cold water. Make the Sugared Walnut Biscuits (Cookies). Cool and store in an airtight container.

On the day:
Cook the dried beans. Be sure to boil them rapidly for 10 minutes at the start of cooking to destroy any toxins that may be present. When the beans are tender, drain, cool and set aside, covered, in the refrigerator. Make the soda bread. Cook the Plums in Port Wine. Cool, cover and store in the refrigerator. Set the table, do the flowers, select the wines. Chilli con Carne has a powerful flavour and demands a robust young wine such as the famous Hungarian Bikaver or 'Bull's Blood' as it is more commonly known.

To serve at 8 pm:
About 6.00: Open the red wine. Start making the Chilli con Carne. Prepare the vegetables, then proceed as in the recipe, aiming to complete the assembly of the dish and set it to simmer by 6.30.
6.30: Slice the cucumbers for the salad, cover with vinegar and salt and set aside to marinate.
7.30: Check the Chilli con Carne. Drain the cucumber slices and transfer them to a serving bowl. Place 300 ml/½ pint (1¼ cups) of double (heavy) cream in a large bowl and whip it until it stands in soft peaks. Divide the whipped cream in half. To one portion, add the coconut cream and other ingredients required for the salad dressing. Mix gently but thoroughly and then pour the dressing over the cucumber slices. Chill the remaining cream to serve with the plums in port.
8.00: Set out the wine, the soda bread and the salad. Serve the meal.

F · R · E · E · Z · E · R · N · O · T · E · S

Cool, pack and freeze the Chilli con Carne at the end of stage 3. Thaw overnight in the refrigerator. To reheat, bring to the boil and simmer for 20-25 minutes. Add more stock if necessary. Cool, wrap in foil and freeze the Wholemeal Soda Bread. Place in a preheated oven (200°C/400°F), Gas Mark 6 for 45-50 minutes to defrost. Use straight away. Freeze the Sugared Walnut Biscuits at the end of stage 4.

M · E · N · U

· 12 ·

Slimmers' Choice for 6

Yugoslavian Spinach Soup

·

Poached Trout
Stuffed Tomatoes
Radicchio and French Bean Salad

·

Pineapple Sorbet

This menu takes slimming as its theme. In these health-conscious times, there's an even chance that at least one of your guests will be actively trying to lose weight. You may even be slimming yourself.

Calorie Counters

We've created a menu that's reasonably low in calories, high in fibre, and quite delicious. It is sensible without being spartan and there are some indulgences for those of your party whho can afford them.

The meal begins with a spinach soup that owes its silky texture to yogurt, not cream. The Poached Trout that follows has only about 30 calories per 25 g/1 oz so you can afford to splurge on the cream sauce. Dedicated dieters can pass this up – if they have the willpower!

Serve the trout with Stuffed Tomatoes and a Radicchio and French Bean Salad. The salad has an oil and garlic dressing which will be taboo to serious slimmers. For this reason we suggest you serve individual portions. Offer the dressing separately, with pure lemon juice or white wine vinegar as alternatives.

Sorbet (sherbet) is always popular and you can enjoy this one in the knowledge that each portion has only about 110 calories.

Yugoslavian Spinach Soup

Metric/Imperial

500 g/1 lb spinach
1 medium onion, finely
  chopped
1 tablespoon oil
2 tablespoons ground
  almonds
125 g/4 oz long-grain
  brown rice
1 litre/1¾ pints chicken
  stock
salt
freshly ground black pepper
1-2 tablespoons chopped dill
300 ml/½ pint natural
  yogurt
chopped cucumber, to
  garnish

American

1 lb spinach
1 medium onion, finely
  chopped
1 tablespoon oil
2 tablespoons finely ground
  almonds
½ cup long-grain brown
  rice
4¼ cups chicken stock
salt
freshly ground black pepper
1-2 tablespoons chopped dill
1¼ cups unflavored yogurt
chopped cucumber, for
  garnish

1. Wash the spinach and discard any tough stalks (stems). Coarsely shred the leaves.
2. Heat the oil in a large saucepan, sauté the onion until nearly tender, then add the ground almonds and cook over low heat until a delicate brown colour. Stir in the rice and blend with the onion and almonds.
3. Pour in the stock, bring to the boil, reduce the heat and simmer for 15 minutes.
4. Add the spinach and simmer for 15 to 20 minutes more or until the rice is tender. Allow to cool slightly, then purée in a blender or food processor.
5. Return the soup to the pan. Add salt, pepper, dill and yogurt. Heat gently. Garnish with cucumber.
·2·7·

Cook's Tip

If using frozen leaf or chopped spinach allow 350 g/ 12 oz (¾ lb) only.

Yugoslavian spinach soup

Poached Trout

Metric/Imperial	American
4 medium rainbow trout, cleaned	4 medium rainbow trout, cleaned
250 ml/8 fl oz dry cider	1 cup hard cider
a few sprigs of parsley	a few sprigs of parsley
1 large onion, sliced	1 large onion, sliced
3 slices of lemon	3 slices of lemon
9 black peppercorns	9 black peppercorns
250 ml/8 fl oz double cream	1 cup heavy cream
salt	salt
freshly ground black pepper	freshly ground black pepper
parsley, to garnish	parsley, for garnish

1. Place the trout in a large shallow pan big enough to hold all the fish in one layer. Add the cider, parsley, onion, lemon and peppercorns. Cover the pan and simmer the fish for 10 to 12 minutes, until they are just cooked.
2. Carefully transfer the poached trout to a serving platter and keep warm while you make the sauce.
3. Strain the poaching liquid into a small pan and bring it rapidly to the boil. Immediately lower the heat, stir in the cream and just heat through. Remove from the heat and season the sauce.
4. Pour the sauce over the fish and garnish with parsley. Serve immediately. ·2·8·

Stuffed Tomatoes

Metric/Imperial	American
6 large firm ripe tomatoes	6 large firm ripe tomatoes
salt	salt
Stuffing:	Stuffing:
1½ tablespoons butter	1½ tablespoons butter
1 small onion, finely chopped	1 small onion, finely chopped
75 g/3 oz fresh wholemeal breadcrumbs	1½ cups soft wholewheat bread crumbs
2 tablespoons flaked almonds	2 tablespoons slivered almonds
½ teaspoon basil	½ teaspoon basil
1 teaspoon tomato purée	1 teaspoon tomato paste
25 g/1 oz grated Parmesan cheese	¼ cup grated Parmesan cheese

1. Cut each tomato in half. Using a spoon, scoop out the pulp and seeds. Finely chop the pulp and set it aside. Salt the hollowed-out tomatoes and turn them upside down on a plate to drain. Leave for at least 35 to 40 minutes.
2. Make the stuffing. Melt the butter in a small pan and fry the onion for 3 to 5 minutes until soft. Stir in the breadcrumbs, almonds and basil and add enough of the chopped tomato pulp to make a moist but still firm stuffing. Stir in the tomato purée (paste).
3. Fill each tomato shell, mounding the stuffing up, and sprinkle a little Parmesan on top of each shell.
4. Arrange the stuffed tomatoes in a buttered ovenproof dish and bake in a preheated oven (190°C/375°F), Gas Mark 5 for 30 minutes. Serve immediately.

Radicchio and French Bean Salad

Metric/Imperial	American
350 g/12 oz French beans	¾ lb green beans
salt	salt
1 head of radicchio	1 head radicchio
1 onion, sliced into rings	1 onion, sliced into rings
2 cloves garlic, peeled and crushed	2 cloves garlic, peeled and crushed
4-5 tablespoons olive oil	¼-¾ cup olive oil

1. Parboil the beans in boiling salted water for 2 minutes, then immediately plunge into iced water to arrest further cooking. Drain and cut into 5 cm/ 2 inch lengths.

2. Wash and dry the radicchio leaves, tear them into manageable pieces and place in a single large salad bowl or in six individual salad bowls with the beans and onion rings.
3. Make the dressing. Beat the garlic with the olive oil and a pinch of salt. Serve the dressing in a small glass jug (pitcher) so that each guest can dress his own salad.

Pineapple Sorbet

Metric/Imperial	American
1 × 382 g/13½ oz can crushed pineapple	1 × 14 oz can crushed pineapple
50 g/2 oz soft brown sugar	¼ cup light brown sugar
1 tablespoon lemon juice	1 tablespoon lemon juice
300 ml/½ pint natural yogurt	1¼ cups unflavored yogurt

1. Drain the pineapple. Reserve the fruit and pour the juice into a large pan. Add the sugar and lemon juice and heat until dissolved. Leave to cool and then stir in the yogurt.
2. Pour into a shallow rigid container and freeze until the mixture is mushy.
3. Remove from the freezer and stir in the crushed pineapple. Return to a rigid container, cover and freeze until solid.
4. Transfer the sorbet (sherbet) to the refrigerator about 1 hour before serving. Spoon into individual sundae dishes to serve.

C · O · U · N · T · D · O · W · N

The day before:
Make the sorbet (sherbet). Store in a shallow rigid container in the freezer.

On the day:
Clean the trout, wrap and store in the refrigerator. Halve the tomatoes, sprinkle with salt and place upside down on a plate to drain. Make the stuffing and store, covered, in the refrigerator. Make the salad dressing, cover and set aside at room temperature. Make the soup up to the end of stage 4. Cool, cover and store in a cool place. Lay the table, do the flowers, select the wines. Serve a rich white wine with the trout, such as Meursault or Graves. Remember to have chilled sparkling spring water available too.

7.00: Chill the wine. Wash the radicchio leaves. Dry between sheets of absorbent kitchen paper. Blanch the beans and slice the onion. Make up six individual salads, cover with cling film (plastic wrap) and chill. Stuff the tomatoes. Top each with Parmesan and arrange them in a buttered ovenproof dish. Cover with clingfilm and store in the refrigerator until required.

7.25: Preheat the oven to (190°C/375°F), Gas Mark 5. Slice the onion and lemon for the trout dish, wrap each in cling film and set aside until required. Remove the sorbet from the freezer and place in the refrigerator.

7.40: Finish making the soup: add the seasoning, dill and half the yogurt and reheat gently. The soup should be thoroughly heated but must not be allowed to boil.

7.45: Pop the tomatoes into the oven to bake.

7.50: Toast the wholemeal (wholewheat) bread and prepare the soup garnish. Set out the ingredients for the trout dish.

8.00: Start poaching the trout. Take the wine to the table and set out the spring water. Garnish the soup and serve.

Between the courses: Drain the trout, cover and keep warm in a low oven while you make the sauce. Garnish before serving. Remove the tomatoes from the oven and serve hot with the trout and salads. Spoon the sorbet into six sundae dishes just before you are ready to serve.

F · R · E · E · Z · E · R · N · O · T · E · S
Only the Pineapple Sorbet (Sherbert) can be stored in the freezer. Store for up to 3 months.

MENU

· 13 ·

Winter Curry Supper for 4

Mixed Vegetable Curry
Brown Rice Pilaf
Broccoli Salad

·

Lattice Apple Tart

There's something comforting about a curry. We know of no better way of banishing the cold on a wet winter's night than by combining curry and good company.

Impromptu Entertaining

Ours is vegetable-based and can be made in the time it takes to prepare the brown rice that accompanies it. It is the ideal dish for a casual supper after work, when energy is at a low ebb and time is short. And because vegetables are almost always available (especially if you grow your own) this is the perfect recipe to have in your repertoire for those dinner invitations you issue on the spur of the moment. The choice of vegetables can be varied according to what is seasonal and you can also include storecupboard items like canned kidney beans or chick peas. We suggest serving the curry with a Brown Rice Pilaf, and a Broccoli Salad but any of the conventional curry sambals would be appropriate.

Table Dressing

Keep the atmosphere casual and welcoming. Use a bold, coarse-textured cloth on the table (or experiment with a bedspread or curtain). Brass trays and bowls would look lovely but use them with inner china dishes and bowls to avoid contamination of the food.

Mixed Vegetable Curry

Metric/Imperial

2 tablespoons oil
250 g/8 oz onions, sliced
1 clove garlic, peeled and
  crushed
1 cooking apple, peeled,
  cored and chopped
2.5 cm/1 inch piece fresh
  root ginger, peeled and
  grated
1 tablespoon mustard seeds
1-2 tablespoons curry
  powder
450 ml/3/4 pint vegetable
  stock
finely grated rind and juice
  of 1/2 lemon
salt
freshly ground black pepper
250 g/8 oz potatoes, diced
250 g/8 oz carrots, sliced
250 g/8 oz tomatoes,
  skinned and roughly
  chopped
250 g/8 oz cauliflower
  florets
250 g/8 oz runner beans,
  sliced
50 g/2 oz sultanas
50 g/2 oz shelled Brazil
  nuts
1 tablespoon grated fresh
  coconut

American

2 tablespoons oil
1/2 lb onions, sliced
1 clove garlic, peeled and
  crushed
1 tart apple, pared, cored
  and chopped
1 inch piece fresh ginger
  root, pared and grated
1 tablespoon mustard seeds
1-2 tablespoons curry
  powder
2 cups vegetable stock
finely grated rind and juice
  of 1/2 lemon
salt
freshly ground black pepper
1 1/3 cups diced raw potato
1 1/2 cups sliced carrots
1 cup peeled and roughly
  chopped tomatoes
2 cups cauliflower flowerets
1 cup sliced snake beans
1/3 cup golden raisins
1/2 cup shelled Brazil nuts
1 tablespoon grated fresh
  coconut

1. Heat the oil in a large saucepan. Add the onions, garlic, apple and ginger and sauté gently for 5 minutes, stirring occasionally. Stir in the mustard seeds and cover the pan. Fry gently until you hear the seeds pop, shaking the pan constantly. Stir in the curry powder and cook for 2 minutes.

2. Add the stock and bring the liquid to the boil, stirring constantly until the sauce thickens slightly. Add the lemon rind and juice and salt and pepper to taste, then reduce the heat and simmer for 2 minutes.

3. Add the potatoes, carrots and tomatoes. Cover the pan and simmer for 10 minutes.

4. Add the cauliflower, beans, sultanas (golden raisins) and nuts. Cover and simmer for a further 10 minutes, or until the vegetables are tender but still crisp and not broken up.

5. Taste and adjust the seasoning. Sprinkle with the coconut and serve hot.

Cook's Tip:

If you prefer to make your own curry powder, combine 1 teaspoon each of ground turmeric, coriander and cumin and add 1/2 teaspoon ground fenugreek and 1/4 teaspoon chilli powder.

Brown Rice Pilaf

Metric/Imperial

2 tablespoons oil
2 medium onions, finely
  chopped
250 g/8 oz long-grain
  brown rice
600 ml/1 pint chicken or
  vegetable stock
1 tablespoon mushroom
  ketchup
salt
freshly ground black pepper

American

2 tablespoons oil
2 medium onions, finely
  chopped
1 cup long-grain brown rice
2 1/2 cups chicken or
  vegetable stock
1 tablespoon mushroom
  ketchup
salt
freshly ground black pepper

1. Heat the oil in a large saucepan, add the onions and sauté for about 5 minutes, until the onions are golden. Stir in the rice and cook over gentle heat for 3 minutes more.

2. Stir in the stock and mushroom ketchup and bring the liquid to the boil.

3. Reduce the heat to very low, cover the pan and simmer for 40 minutes, by which time all the liquid should have been absorbed. If necessary, remove the lid and increase the heat to dry off any excess liquid.
4. Season the rice with salt and pepper, fork it through and transfer it to a platter to serve.

Broccoli Salad

Metric/Imperial	American
750 g/1½ lb broccoli, fresh or frozen, cut into 2.5 cm/1 inch lengths	1½ lb broccoli, fresh or frozen, cut into 1 inch lengths
salt	salt
50 g/2 oz button mushrooms, thinly sliced	½ cup thinly sliced button mushrooms
1 tablespoon walnut halves	1 tablespoon walnut halves

Dressing:
1 tablespoon olive oil
1 teaspoon orange juice
1 teaspoon white wine
  vinegar
½ teaspoon honey
salt
freshly ground black pepper

Dressing:
1 tablespoon olive oil
1 teaspoon orange juice
1 teaspoon white wine
  vinegar
½ teaspoon honey
salt
freshly ground black pepper

1. First make the dressing. Combine all the ingredients in a small jar. Whisk or shake well to combine thoroughly.
2. Cook the fresh or frozen broccoli in boiling salted water until it is just tender. Immediately plunge into iced water to arrest further cooking. Drain and

Lattice apple tart

arrange in a shallow serving dish. Pour over the dressing and cover with cling film (plastic wrap). Chill in the refrigerator until required.

3. About 15 minutes before serving, add the mushrooms and toss lightly. Chill in the refrigerator until required.

4. Garnish with walnuts to serve. ·10·

Lattice Apple Tart

Metric/Imperial	American
250 g/8 oz Wholemeal Pastry (see page 28)	1/2 lb Wholewheat Pastry (see page 28)
4 large cooking apples, peeled, cored and sliced	4 large tart apples, pared, cored and sliced
75 g/3 oz raisins	1/2 cup raisins
25 g/1 oz hazelnuts, roughly chopped	1/4 cup hazelnuts, roughly chopped
25 g/1 oz soft brown sugar	2 tablespoons light brown sugar
1 teaspoon cinnamon	1 teaspoon ground cinnamon
25 g/1 oz butter	2 tablespoons butter
milk for brushing	milk for brushing

1. Roll out the pastry. Line a 23 cm/9 inch pie dish. Trim the pastry edges. Reserve the trimmings.
2. Arrange the apples and raisins evenly over the pie shell and sprinkle with nuts, sugar and cinnamon. Dot the top with butter and add 3 tablespoons water.
3. Roll out the pastry trimmings and cut into strips. Arrange in a lattice over the tart, wetting the pastry ends to stick. Brush with milk.
4. Bake in a preheated oven (200°C/400°F), Gas Mark 6 for 30 to 35 minutes, until the pastry is golden brown and the apples are tender. ·9·

C · O · U · N · T · D · O · W · N
On the day:
If you prefer to make your own curry powder, do it now. Make the pastry for the apple tart, wrap and

chill. Make the Broccoli Salad up to the end of stage 2. Lay the table, do the flowers, select the drinks. Beer goes well with curry. Serve it well chilled. If you prefer wine, choose a semi-sweet white wine such as a Californian Chenin Blanc or a Rhine Spätlese. Again, serve the wine well chilled.

To serve at 8 pm:
6.00: Chill the beer or white wine.
6.10: Preheat the oven to (200°C/400°F), Gas Mark 6. Prepare the apples for the tart, slicing them into cold acidulated water.
6.30: Roll out the pastry and make the apple tart. Bake it for 30 to 35 minutes.
7.00: Prepare the vegetables for the curry. Start cooking the pilaf.
7.25: Start cooking the curry.
7.30: Check the pilaf. The heat should be gentle enough to prevent the rice sticking to the bottom of the pan.
7.40: Add the potatoes, carrots and tomatoes to the curry. Simmer for 10 minutes.
7.45: Add the mushrooms to the Broccoli Salad and toss.
7.50: Add the cauliflower, beans, sultanas (golden raisins) and nuts to the curry, cover and simmer until ready to serve. Check the pilaf.
8.00: Serve the curry and rice, together with the cucumber raita. Garnish the Broccoli Salad with walnuts and serve.

F · R · E · E · Z · E · R · N · O · T · E · S
Cool, pack and freeze the Mixed Vegetable Curry at the end of stage 5. Thaw overnight at cool room temperature. Place in an ovenproof dish. Cover and reheat in a preheated oven (200°C/400°F), Gas Mark 6 for 45 minutes.

Cool, pack and freeze the Lattice Apple Tart at the end of stage 4. Thaw overnight at cool room temperature. Cover with foil and refresh in a preheated oven (200°C/400°F), Gas Mark 6 for 15 to 20 minutes.

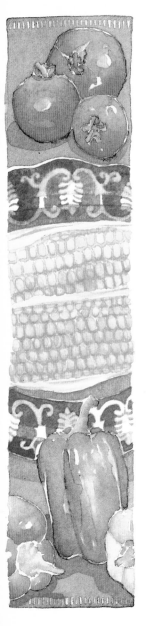

⸝ᵒM·E·N·U⸝ᵒ

· 14 ·

Teenage Supper for 6

Hummus

·

Sausages with Broccoli
Jacket Potatoes with Cottage Cheese and Walnuts
Oriental Mange Tout Salad

·

Redcurrant Tansy

Teenagers have an ambivalent attitude to food. On the one hand they are usually aware of the importance of healthy eating habits and may, for instance, insist upon starting each day with a carrot juice and wheatgerm flip; but on the other hand they generally like their food to be recognizable and reasonably familiar.

Easy to Eat

This menu is therefore something of a compromise. The Hummus may be an unknown quantity to some of the guests, but it is tasty and easy to eat and serving it as a dip with wholemeal (wholewheat) bread means that each guest can have as much (or as little) as he likes!

The main course stars sausages, which are sure to appeal, and we've added jacket potatoes (cottage cheese plus walnuts for extra fibre).

Prepare Ahead

Most of the dishes can be prepared well in advance of the evening, and the teenagers should be able to do much of the cooking themselves. It's best to let them set the scene for the evening, too. Their ideas on appropriate decor are bound to be at variance with your own!

Hummus

Metric/Imperial	American
125 g/4 oz chick peas	1/2 cup chick peas
600 ml/1 pint water	2 1/2 cups water
150 ml/1/4 pint natural yogurt	2/3 cup unflavored yogurt
2 tablespoons lemon juice	2 tablespoons lemon juice
3 tablespoons tahini (sesame seed paste) or peanut butter	3 tablespoons tahini (sesame seed paste) or peanut butter
1 clove garlic, peeled and crushed	1 clove garlic, peeled and crushed
salt	salt
freshly ground black pepper	freshly ground black pepper
paprika, to serve	paprika, to serve

1. Soak the chick peas in the water overnight. Drain. Transfer the chick peas to a saucepan, adding fresh water.
2. Cover and bring to the boil. Boil for 10 minutes, then reduce the heat and simmer for 1 to 1 1/2 hours, adding more water if necessary, until the chick peas are soft enough to mash.
3. Drain the chick peas, reserving the cooking liquid.
4. Mash the chick peas with 2 tablespoons of the cooking liquid. Beat in the yogurt, lemon juice, tahini or peanut butter, garlic and salt and pepper to taste. Alternatively place all the ingredients in a blender or food processor and purée. Thin with a little more of the cooking liquid if necessary. Sprinkle with paprika. Serve with wholemeal (wholewheat) rolls. ·2·

Sausages with Brocoli

Metric/Imperial	American
2 tablespoons vegetable oil	2 tablespoons vegetable oil
2 cloves garlic, peeled and crushed	2 cloves garlic, peeled and crushed
1 × 70 g/2 3/4 oz can pimentos, drained and chopped	1 × 3 oz can pimentos, drained and chopped
750 g/1 1/2 lb Italian Salamelle or pork sausages	1 1/2 lb Italian Salamelle or pork sausage links
salt	salt
freshly ground black pepper	freshly ground black pepper
750 g/1 1/2 lb fresh broccoli, trimmed	1 1/2 lb fresh broccoli, trimmed

1. Heat the oil in a flameproof casserole, add the garlic and sauté gently until soft.
2. Add the pimento to the pan, together with the sausages and salt and pepper to taste. Fry for about 3 minutes.
3. Cover the casserole and transfer it to a preheated oven (190°C/375°F), Gas Mark 5. Bake for about 45 minutes until the sausages are cooked.
4. Meanwhile cook the broccoli in boiling salted water until tender. Drain and place in a warm serving dish. Add the sausages. Serve hot.

Jacket Potatoes with Cottage Cheese and Walnuts

Metric/Imperial	American
6 large potatoes, scrubbed but not peeled	6 large potatoes, scrubbed but not peeled
salt to taste	salt to taste
300 g/10 oz cottage cheese	1 1/4 cups cottage cheese
125 g/4 oz walnuts, chopped	1 cup chopped walnuts

1. Cook and cut the potatoes, following stages 1 and 2 of the recipe for Jacket Potatoes with Yogurt and Chives (see page 27).
2. Combine the cottage cheese and walnuts and divide the mixture between the potatoes.

Oriental Mange Tout Salad

Metric/Imperial
650 g/1 ¼ lb mange tout
salt
250 g/8 oz button
mushrooms, sliced
1 small red pepper, cored,
seeded and finely chopped
2 tablespoons sesame seeds
Dressing:
3 tablespoons sunflower oil
1 tablespoon soy sauce
1-2 tablespoons lemon juice
1 tablespoon brown sugar
(optional)

American
1 ¼ lb snow peas, cleaned
salt
2 cups thinly sliced button
mushrooms
1 small red pepper, seeded
and finely chopped
2 tablespoons sesame seeds
Dressing:
3 tablespoons sunflower oil
1 tablespoon soy sauce
1-2 tablespoons lemon juice
1 tablespoon brown sugar
(optional)

Oriental mange tout salad

1. String the mange tout if necessary. Add them to a pan of boiling salted water, return to the boil, reduce the heat and simmer for 1 minute. Immediately plunge them into iced water to arrest further cooking. Drain and set aside.
2. Make the dressing. Combine all the ingredients in a large mixing bowl, adding lemon juice to taste and sugar if a sweet dressing is preferred. Add the sugar gradually and taste between each addition.
3. Toss the mushrooms in the dressing until thoroughly coated. Add the red pepper, together with the drained mange tout, and toss again.
4. To serve, turn into one large or several small bowls and sprinkle with the sesame seeds.

Redcurrant Tansy

Metric/Imperial	American
500 g/1 lb redcurrants, stalks removed	1 lb red currants, stems removed
125 g/4 oz soft brown sugar	2/3 cup, packed, light brown sugar
3 egg yolks	3 egg yolks
1 tablespoon caster sugar	1 tablespoon superfine sugar
2 teaspoons cornflour	2 teaspoons cornstarch
300 ml/1/2 pint milk	1 1/4 cups milk
150 ml/1/4 pint double cream, whipped, to serve	2/3 cup heavy cream, whipped, to serve

1. Put the redcurrants in a saucepan with the brown sugar and simmer gently for 8 to 10 minutes until soft. Leave to cool, then purée in a blender or food processor or pass through a nylon sieve (strainer).
2. Put the egg yolks, caster (superfine) sugar and cornflour (cornstarch) in a bowl and beat until thoroughly blended.
3. Bring the milk to the boil in a small pan and then stir it into the egg mixture. Strain the custard mixture into the top of a double boiler or a heatproof bowl over a pan of simmering water and cook gently, stirring constantly, until the sauce will coat the back of a spoon.
4. Remove from the heat and fold in the redcurrant purée. Leave to cool, stirring occasionally.
5. When cold, beat the redcurrant mixture, then carefully fold in the whipped cream with a metal spoon to create a marbled effect. Spoon the tansy into six individual glasses and chill in the refrigerator until required. Serve chilled with Sugared Walnut Biscuits (see page 48).

C · O · U · N · T · D · O · W · N

Two days before:
Soak the chick peas for the Hummus.

The day before:
Make the Hummus, spoon it into one large or several small serving dishes and refrigerate, tightly covered, until required.

On the day:
Make the mange tout salad, cover and chill until needed. Make the Redcurrant Tansy. Lay the table, do the flowers (check with teenagers first as they may well scorn this idea). Set out the drinks. A fruit punch may prove popular. If your teenage host or hostess approves of this, make it now. Cover and refrigerate until required.

To serve at 8 pm:
6.55: Preheat the oven to (190°C/375°F), Gas Mark 5. Scrub the jacket potatoes.
7.00: Crush the garlic and chop the pimientos for the sausage dish. Trim the broccoli. Make the sausage dish up to the end of stage 2.
7.15: Put the sausage dish into the centre of the oven with the jacket potatoes on the shelf above.
7.45: Cook the broccoli in a large pan of boiling salted water for 12 to 15 minutes, or until tender. Test the stalks with a skewer. They should be just cooked. Make the filling for the potatoes.
8.00: Drain the broccoli and place it in a warm serving dish. Add the sausages and toss well. Keep warm until required. Serve the Hummus with wholemeal rolls.
Between courses: Make a cross in each baked potato and top each with filling. Toss the salad.

F · R · E · E · Z · E · R · N · O · T · E · S
Pack and freeze the Redcurrant Tansy at the end of stage 5. Thaw overnight in the refrigerator. Stir lightly before serving.

Variation:
If mange tout are not available for the Oriental Mange Tout salad, young French (green) beans may be used instead. Blanch them for 3 to 5 minutes.

Cook's Tip:
The Hummus may be served with warm pitta bread fingers. Place 3 pitta breads in a hot oven for 10 minutes. Cut into 2.5 cm/1 inch finger lengths.

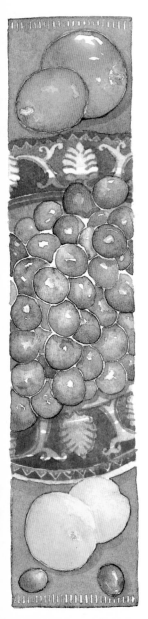

· 15 ·

Chinese Meal for 4

Sweet and Sour Chicken
Stir-fried Bean Sprouts

·

Sweet Peanut Cream

Instead of nipping out for a Chinese takeaway, why not nip in for one? Here's a simple Chinese meal that can be put together in less time than it would take you to trot to the takeaway.

A wok makes short work of stir-frying, but if you do not have one a heavy-based frying pan (skillet) will do instead.

At the Ready

The essential thing to remember is that your preparations must be thorough. Seconds count in stir-frying so before you start, line up all your ingredients within easy reach. If you've ever watched a TV cook, you'll know the best way of doing this. Group ingredients for each dish separately and make sure you've forgotten nothing. Even small amounts, such as 1 tablespoon of soy sauce, should be spooned onto a saucer ready for use. The cooking will take all your concentration, so don't leave anything to luck.

Prepare the vegetables as late as possible before cooking, to minimise vitamin loss. Serve pre-dinner drinks in the kitchen and have your guests chat to you while you work. Better still, have them work while you chat!

The cooking is all done at the last minute, which means you will have one or two pans to attend to simultaneously. Enlist the help of your partner or one of your guests if you find the thought of this rather daunting – and put another guest in charge of the wines.

Sweet and Sour Chicken

Metric/Imperial
50 g/1½ oz butter
1 onion, coarsely chopped
2 teaspoons cornflour
1 × 227 g/8 oz can
  pineapple chunks
1 tablespoon soy sauce
1 tablespoon vinegar
2 carrots, thinly sliced
1 teaspoon sugar
Batter:
125 g/4 oz plain flour,
  sifted
pinch of salt
1 egg, beaten
600 ml/1 pint milk

American
3 tablespoons butter
1 onion, coarsely chopped
2 teaspoons cornstarch
1 × 8 oz can pineapple
  chunks
1 tablespoon soy sauce
1 tablespoon vinegar
2 carrots, thinly sliced
1 teaspoon sugar
Batter:
1 cup all-purpose flour,
  sifted
pinch of salt
1 egg, beaten
2½ cups milk

125 g/4 oz cooked chicken,
  cut into pieces
boiled rice, to serve

¼ lb cooked chicken, cut
  into pieces
boiled rice, to serve

1. To make the batter combine the flour, salt, egg and milk and whisk. Leave to stand.
2. Sauté onions in butter until soft. Add cornflour. Stir in the cornflour (cornstarch).
3. Drain the pineapple chunks, reserving the juice. Make the juice up to 450 ml/¾ pint (2 cups) with the soy sauce, vinegar and water, then add to the pan.
4. Bring the mixture to the boil, add carrot, pineapple and sugar, cover and simmer for 20 minutes.
5. Dip the chicken pieces into the batter and coat. Deep-fry until golden brown.
6. Put the boiled rice on a warmed serving dish. Top with the chicken and pour the sauce over.

Stir-fried Bean Sprouts

Metric/Imperial	American
3 tablespoons sesame seed oil	3 tablespoons sesame seed oil
1 onion, finely chopped	1 onion, finely chopped
350 g/12 oz fresh bean sprouts	6 cups fresh bean sprouts
125 g/4 oz bamboo shoots, sliced	½ cup sliced bamboo shoots
2 celery sticks, diagonally sliced	2 celery stalks, diagonally sliced
a little lemon juice	a little lemon juice
salt	salt
freshly ground black pepper	freshly ground black pepper

1. Heat the oil in a wok or heavy-based frying pan (skillet) and stir-fry the onion for 1 minute.
2. Add the bean sprouts, bamboo shoots and celery and stir-fry for 4 minutes more.
3. Remove from the heat and add a little lemon juice and salt and pepper to taste. Serve immediately.

Sweet Peanut Cream

Metric/Imperial	American
50 g/2 oz smooth peanut butter	¼ cup smooth peanut butter
1 litre/1¾ pints milk or water	4 cups milk or water
50 g/2 oz soft brown sugar	⅓ cup light brown sugar
4 teaspoons rice flour or cornflour, mixed with 4 tablespoons water	4 teaspoons rice flour or cornstarch, mixed with ¼ cup water

1. Put the peanut butter in a saucepan and gradually stir in the milk or water to make a smooth paste. Add the sugar and bring to the boil, stirring constantly. The mixture should remain smooth and creamy.

Sweet and sour chicken

2. Add the rice flour or cornflour (cornstarch) mixture and cook, stirring, until the mixture thickens.
3. Transfer to a serving bowl and serve immediately or cover the surface closely with cling film (plastic wrap) and leave to cool. Reheat the Sweet Peanut Cream very gently in a double boiler when required and serve warm.

Cook's Tip:
Offer a bowl of fresh lychees with this dessert. The two make an interesting and unusual combination.

C · O · U · N · T · D · O · W · N

On the day:
Make the Sweet Peanut Cream. Cool, cover closely with cling film (plastic wrap) and refrigerate. Lay the table, do the flowers and set out the wine. Serve a dry to medium dry white wine for preference. Try a Californian Pinot Blanc or an Italian Orvieto. Well chilled of course.

To serve at about 8 pm:
6.00: Make the batter. Make the sweet and sour sauce.
6.30: Chill the white wine. Remove the peanut cream from the refrigerator.
6.45: Prepare the vegetables for the Stir-fried Bean sprouts and combine them on a second platter. Cover with cling film and refrigerate.
7.15: Set out the ingredients for the Chinese dishes in separate groups. Have the pans ready.
7.50: Start cooking the meal. In one pan cook the Sweet and Sour Chicken. In a second pan fry the bean sprout dish. As soon as all the dishes are cooked, serve the meal. Don't forget the wines.
Between courses: Transfer the peanut cream to the top of a double boiler set over simmering water and reheat gently, stirring constantly, until warm. Serve immediately.

F · R · E · E · Z · E · R · N · O · T · E · S
None of the dishes is suitable for freezing.

I · N · D · E · X

A·C·K·N·O·W·L·E·D·G·E·M·E·N·T·S

Theo Bergstrom 31, 39; Californian Raisin Information Service 55; Laurie Evans 43, 50, 59; Robert Golden 19, 23; James Jackson 34; Paul Kemp 46, Roger Phillips 14; Rice Council 62; Clive Streeter 11; Paul Williams 7, 27.

Jacket photography: Clive Streeter   Illustration: Alison Wisenfeld